THE
GALÁPAGOS
ISLANDS

THE
GALÁPAGOS
ISLANDS

A SPIRITUAL JOURNEY

BRIAN D. McLAREN

Fortress Press
Minneapolis

THE GALÁPAGOS ISLANDS
A Spiritual Journey

Print ISBN: 978-1-5064-4825-1
eBook ISBN: 978-1-5064-4826-8

You can see my photographs from the trip by going to
brianmclaren.net/galapagosphotos. Thanks to Julie Pelletier (p.
82), my Swiss travel companions (p. 120), and Ron Dunn (p. 172)
for use of their photos included in this book. All other photos are
courtesy of my iPhone 7.

Cover image: Thang Tat Nguyen; getty images /moment collection
Cover design: Drew Design
Map illustration: Paul Soupiset

DEDICATION

This book is dedicated to my father, Dr. Ian D. McLaren (1924–2014). He loved the outdoors, and he was always ready for an adventure. How many mountain trails did I hike, lakes did I canoe across, impromptu picnics did I enjoy, and crackling campfires did I help build because of his contagious energy and love for life? My life has overflowed with so much joy because he was my dad.

This book is also dedicated to my friend and mentor, Fr. Richard Rohr, OFM. He teaches that creation is the original Bible, and he knows that the door that opens outward into creation also leads us inward into holy contemplation.

Finally, this book is dedicated to my grandson, Lucas McLaren Stone, who inherited my love for all things alive. I smile to think that he will be watching tortoises, listening for birdsongs, and following the flight of dragonflies long after I'm gone. Lucas, his sisters Ella and Ada, and his cousins Averie and Mia inspire me to protect this beautiful earth, for them and for their grandchildren's grandchildren.

CONTENTS

Galápagos
the enchanted islands

WOLF VOLCANO

ECUADOR VOLCANO

DARWIN VOLCANO

ALCEDO VOLCANO

URBINA BAY

FERNANDINA

JAMES BAY (north coast)

SANTIAGO

BALTRA

la Golondrina

PUERTO AYORA

SANTA CRUZ

SIERRA NEGRA

PUERTO VILLAMIL

CERRO AZUL

ISABELA

N

PACIFIC OCEAN

PREFACE:
SITUATION

This book entered my life as a surprise, a needed surprise in an unpleasant situation.

My friend Tony Jones, an insightful theologian, gifted writer, and skilled editor at Fortress Press, contacted me with an idea. He was planning a series of books that would be one part travel guide, one part spiritual memoir, and one part ethical/theological reflection. Would I be willing to launch the series, he asked, with a book on the Galápagos Islands?

"I can't pay you an advance," he said, "but I can cover your expenses."

"Let me think about it and get back to you," I replied. But I didn't need much convincing.

I immediately thought of Anthony Bourdain, vigorously alive then, but gone a few months later. Bourdain's show *Parts Unknown* delighted millions by bringing together travel and a love for food. Similarly, the late Steve Irwin's show *The Crocodile Hunter* combined travel with a love for interacting with wildlife. Why not combine travel with a love for justice, compassion, goodness, wonder, and God? Tony's idea made perfect sense to me.

After all, from Exodus to the story of the prodigal son, the spiritual life has been understood as a journey. The Gospels and Acts read as travel stories following Jesus around Palestine and Paul around the Mediterranean. Even today, people love reading tweets and blog posts about twenty-first-century experiences on the Camino de Santiago, just as they loved to read *Canterbury Tales* in the fourteenth century. Spirituality and travel have a long history of going together.

So as an avid traveler with deep spiritual commitments, this assignment felt like a good fit for me personally.

It felt like a good fit professionally as well.

For the last twenty years, I've been writing about the postmodern/postcolonial turn and the challenges and opportunities it presents to people of faith, and especially Christians. This turn, among other things, involves a recognition that behind every statement there is a story, a story of struggle and joy, quest and conquest, oppression and liberation, predicament and opportunity. And every story has a setting, so settings matter.

The postmodern turn challenges us to see from the start that all theology and spirituality (like all politics, economics, and other human endeavors) are situated, with all the limitations and benefits being situated brings. Where you do your theology and where you practice your spirituality will have a profound effect on you and the outcome of your endeavors. If you live on a farm in a tropical setting, you will experience the world and life and God differently from people who spend their lives in a refugee camp in a harsh desert, at a trading outpost above the Arctic Circle, or on the twenty-sixth floor of an urban skyscraper. "Every viewpoint is a view from a point," a postmodern mantra says, which doesn't mean (as is often accused) that everything is equally true (or false) but rather that every person or group sees and speaks from a perspective, a situation.

> **Travel is still the most intense mode of learning.**
>
> — Kevin Kelly

Each situation has advantages and disadvantages. If you engage in theology and spiritual practice from a situation of power and privilege at the top of the social and economic pyramid, for example, you will see what's visible from that lofty perspective, but you will miss a lot too. If you work from a situation of oppression and struggle at the bottom, lugging the bricks to build the pyramid upon which elites are perched, you will see things from that perspective that those at the top can't imagine.[1]

Similarly, spiritual and theological work done in solitude will differ from work done in community, and homogenous or authoritarian communities will likely produce conclusions that differ greatly from work done in communities of diversity and freedom. It's not that one situation is purely good and all others are bad, but rather, that all situations are simultaneously unique and limited, which argues for all of us to listen to people who see and speak from different situations and, when possible, to put ourselves in different situations through travel.

---

1. I should add that as a privileged straight white male in America, I only came to this understanding slowly and through the influence of writers and thinkers who came from very different social locations. As my book *Everything Must Change* (Grand Rapids: Zondervan, 2007) makes clear, my most important (and often least popular) insights have come through travel to slums, squatter areas, refugee camps, and other places where "the empire" dumps or ignores what it considers trash. From those diverse situations, diverse people could help me see what my inherited situation had effectively hindered me from seeing before. Of course, I still have a lot to learn and unlearn.

> We want to experience the Earth firsthand, to feel the wind on our face, plunge into the mountain waters, enter into virgin forest, and capture the expressions of biodiversity. An attitude of enchantment is resurfacing, a new sense of the sacred is reemerging.
>
> —Leonardo Boff

Meanwhile, our spiritual and theological lives aren't shaped by our social, economic, or cultural location alone. Even our environmental context will influence the kind of theology and spirituality we profess and practice.

Most theology in recent centuries, especially white Christian theology, has been the work of avid indoorsmen, scholars who typically work in square boxes called offices or classrooms or sanctuaries, surrounded by square books and, more recently, square screens, under square roofs in square buildings surrounded by other square buildings, laid out in square city blocks that stretch as far as the eye can see. If practitioners of this civilized indoor theology look out at the world, it is through square windows or in brief moments between the time they exit one square door and enter another. But those outdoor times are generally brief, so these days, this square theology exists almost exclusively in heated and air-conditioned spaces that maintain a pleasant and consistent seventy-two degrees, whatever the season or latitude.

For a long time, this civilized indoor theology was created and promoted almost exclusively by privileged male human beings of European descent, with at least the appearance of heterosexual orientation and physical and mental abilities deemed "normal." Thankfully, more and more people are taking part in civilized indoor theology these days—women, people of color, LGBTQ persons, people of diverse abilities, and others without traditional markers of privilege. But even so, apart from the apocryphal donkeys, sheep, and oxen of the Christmas story, or lambs and bulls being slaughtered in the temple, or the "creeping things" of the first creation account, you'd never know, or hardly need to know, that animals exist, not to mention nonfood plants, flowing rivers, vast oceans, or swirling galaxies.

There is nothing inherently wrong about civilized, indoor theology. Except this: theology that arises in human-made, human-controlled architecture—of walls and mirrors, of doors and locks, of ninety-degree angles and monochrome painted surfaces, of thermostats and plumbing, of politics and prisons, of wars, racism, greed, and fear—will surely reflect the prejudices and limited imaginations of its makers.

It will differ markedly from theology that arises in conversation with the wild world that flourishes beyond our walls and outside our windows and cities. Yes, indoor, civilized theology offers many unique insights from its civilized point of view. But it will miss much and distort much.

So, more and more of us are imagining a wild theology that arises under the stars and planets, along a thundering river or meandering stream, admiring a flock of pelicans or weaver finches, watching a lion stalk a wildebeest, gazing at a spider spinning her web, observing a single tree bud form, swell, burst, and bloom. We imagine a wild theology that doesn't limit itself to Plato and Aquinas but also consults the wisdom of rainbow trout and sea turtles, seasons and tides. We imagine a wild theology whose horizons are measured not by thousands of years and miles but by billions of light years. We imagine a wild theology that is articulated in books, yes, but also in stories and songs, in foods and feasts, in dances and lamentations and pilgrimages that resonate with the turning seasons and rhythmic tides of the natural world.

In all likelihood, it was wild theology that inspired the tribal people to tell the primal stories that were eventually written in the texts that are studied today in heated libraries and interpreted in air-conditioned classrooms.

In all likelihood, wild theology is the mother of civilized theology. And in all likelihood, civilized theology is in the process of killing its mother and acting as if she never existed.

I am a civilized man. I normally live in glass and cement, work among screens and buttons, travel on wheels and immovable metal wings, breathe air-conditioned air and drink chemically treated water as I move from box to box and square to square.

But from my childhood, I have also loved the outdoors. Hiking, camping, kayaking, fly-fishing, birding, gardening, and stargazing are among my greatest joys in life, and these passions have given me a vantage point from which to view indoor, civilized theology with some suspicion. All the more because of the historical and political situation in which I find myself. Like many, I have been heartsick at what's been happening in the so-called civilized world in recent years: environmental insanity and climate-change denial; a resurgence of white supremacy, religious supremacy, and hate crimes; a growing chasm between the majority of us and a tiny minority of super-rich, superpowerful superelites, along with a redistribution of wealth and power in their direction; all while the arms industry distributes increasingly destructive weapons to more and more fearful and resentful people in unstable nations governed by kleptocrats. (Enough said.) When the invitation came to write this book, I needed, far more than I realized, to get away from the dirty churn of cable news and Twitter, to be resituated in the wild, unboxed, outdoor world of creation.

Tony's invitation opened a door to do some wild theology in one of the most unique, beautiful, and important ecological situations in the world. What Jerusalem, Rome, or Mecca might be to civilized theologians, the Galápagos Islands are to wild theologians, for reasons that I hope will become clear in the following pages.

Since returning from my adventure, I was part of a group that spent a half-day in the Twin Cities of Minnesota with Jim Bear Jacobs, a member of the Stockbridge-Munsee

Travel isn't always pretty. It isn't always comfortable. Sometimes it hurts, it even breaks your heart. But that's okay. The journey changes you — it should change you. You take something with you. Hopefully, you leave something good behind.

—Anthony Bourdain *(adapted)*

Mohican Nation, and with Bob Klanderud of the Dakota/ Lakota Nation.[2] Jim Bear said something I had never heard before, something I will never forget. "You people of European descent," he said, "tend to think of events occurring on a timeline. An event that is distant on that timeline is

_____

2. I highly recommend you participate in one of their programs. Learn more at "Healing Minnesota Stories," Minnesota Council of Churches, https://tinyurl.com/yd9c84or.

distant to you. But we indigenous peoples think of events primarily occurring in a place. Whenever we are near that place, we are near that event, no matter when it happened. For us, places hold stories. Places become sacred because of the stories they hold." Then he and Bob walked us through places that held stories that are too seldom told and too often kept secret, stories of what happened to the Native peoples at the hands of the colonizers and settlers, hidden stories that, like hidden wounds, need to be exposed so that healing can come.

> The world is big and I want to have a good look at it before it gets dark.
>
> —John Muir

The Galápagos Islands hold some amazing stories, stories of great importance for the world, especially at a dangerous time when many of our prevailing stories are failing us. I hope that the stories I have brought back from my journey will help you experience healing and become an agent of healing yourself.

I wish the story of this journey could be shared in person around a campfire, told along a trail, sung beside a river, or chanted as poetry on a boat rolling on the waves of the Pacific. Perhaps, as you turn this next page, you can make that be so in your imagination.

INTRODUCTION:
ALMOST THERE

When does a journey begin? Is it when you board the plane or ship or take the first step on the trail? Does it begin when you buy the ticket or choose your date of departure?

Did this journey for me begin this morning when I left my home for the airport?

Or did it begin when I was a little boy of about four?

I lived in Cattaraugus County in upstate New York. Our one-story house sat along a gravel road across from a cow pasture. In one of my earliest and most precious memories, my dad and I are walking hand-in-hand up the gentle slope behind our home, trudging between patches of wet springtime snow, tiny shoots of green breaking through tussocks of gray-brown winter-killed grass. We

1

are heading onto the property of our neighbor, Mr. Eiser. He has a pond we call Eiser's Pond.

In my dad's free hand swings a bright blue plastic bucket. We are on a mission I don't yet understand.

He has noticed on recent nights the sound of frogs and toads calling from the pond. Their squawks and trills spark a memory from his boyhood, and he wants his first-born son to experience it.

We stand on the bank, my dad peering into the newly ice-free water. He kneels and points to a spot in the water. My eyes follow his finger to a mysterious glob of perfectly printed periods, each encased in a sphere of clear jelly, joined together in a clump the size of a young man's fist.

Even now, I see that young man in a plaid 1950s shirt, reaching down with that blue plastic bucket into a stand of cattails, dipping the bucket in the frigid water until the mass of leopard frog eggs plops in over the rim.

We bring the eggs home and put them in a glass bowl. My long-suffering mom allows the bowl to be the centerpiece of the kitchen table for several weeks, much to the delight of my little brother and me.

Gradually, the periods become commas, and the squirming commas turn into tiny tadpoles that wriggle inside their jelly spheres. Finally the spheres grow ragged and the tadpoles emerge, shimmying like tiny, clumsy,

> I urge you: go find buildings and mountains and oceans to swallow you whole. They will save you, in a way nothing else can.
> — Christopher Poindexter

chubby serpents. We feed them lettuce and fish food, and somehow they grow.

When they sprout hind legs, my dad puts a small rock in the bowl. Soon front legs pop out, and then their tails begin to disappear. Their heads and faces take shape, eyes bulging up, tiny round mouths spreading into a wide frog-smile. The froglets climb out on the rock, and when their tails shrink to a stub, we set them free.

Did my parents know that as those tadpoles metamorphosed, I would too? Did they know that gazing into that bowl, I would become a student of the wild, a lover of living things, a disciple of nature, eager for my next outdoor adventure?

From that tender age forward, I was the boy whose favorite pastime was to go to the creek and turn over rocks, wondering at fossils, grabbing crayfish behind their waving upraised pinchers, netting striped silver minnows, finding all manner of salamanders and snakes, curious to know the name of every tree and flower. My childhood pets included cats and a dog, of course, but also rabbits, hamsters, gerbils, parakeets, tropical fish, uncounted garter snakes, a boa constrictor, turtles, salamanders, chipmunks, and an orphaned raccoon.

Even now, sixty years later, I have chosen to live at the intersection of the Everglades and the Gulf of Mexico in Florida, where one wild place meets another. My friends call me a "bird nerd" because I'm still obsessively curious

In the vastness of the Pacific there's a place unlike any other: enchanted volcanic islands that are home to a remarkable collection of animals and plants. Here, evolution is proceeding with spectacular speed. Black lizards that swim in the oceans and spit salt from their noses. Penguins thousands of miles from Antarctica. And an abundance of unique plants.

—David Attenborough

about the name of every bird I hear calling from a nearby thicket. If you visit my backyard, you'll find a small herd of tortoises and turtles wandering beneath a grove of young mango and avocado trees.

My summertime ritual includes volunteering to monitor sea turtle nests, marveling every year at the miraculous cycles of life. If I have a few free hours, I'm out on my kayak, fly-fishing for tarpon and snook and peacock bass, cruising among alligators and an occasional crocodile, paddling with dolphins and manatees, greeting swallow-tailed kites and least terns as my familiar friends and neighbors.

When I was seven, my family moved south to Maryland and my parents often took my brother and me to the National Zoo in Washington, DC. My favorite place at the zoo was the Reptile House, and my favorite display in that warm, humid building was the Galápagos tortoises. Only in my wildest dreams did I imagine I might be able to visit them in their native habitat one day. To do so would be a once-in-a-lifetime trip for sure.

As it happens, this once-in-a-lifetime trip to the Galápagos Islands will be mine to enjoy twice.

If I owe this second Galápagos trip to Tony Jones and Fortress Press, I owe my first trip to my son Trevor and my wife, Grace. When our kids were younger, I made a promise to them: I would take each of them on a trip, anywhere in the world, just the two of us, before they finished high school. My older daughter, Rachel, chose France. My older son, Brett, chose Costa Rica. My younger daughter, Jodi, chose Africa. And Trevor chose the Galápagos. I was a pastor and my salary was modest, but Grace and I had a hunch that this would be one of our best investments, and it certainly was, for my children and for me.

Memories of that 2001 adventure will show up in this story a few times. That trip was all the more meaningful because Trevor, then sixteen years old, was already a cancer survivor. It was a dual celebration of his upcoming graduation from high school and his previous graduation from chemotherapy. Now, seventeen years later, he's a married man with a life full of his own many adventures.

If this second Galápagos voyage is a celebration in any parallel way, it will be a celebration of my own survival, my own graduation, in ways that I feel but do not yet understand, ways that I trust will become clearer to both you and me in the days (and pages) to come. All that's clear to me now is this: I need this trip. I need a break from the toxic politics of my native land. I need to extract myself from the stale indoor air of religious struggle and controversy in which I often find myself as a Christian writer, speaker, and activist. I need to be rebaptized into the wild, natural world outside of confining, man-made boxes. Before I received this invitation, I didn't know how desperately I needed these things, but now, sitting here in this airport, I feel like my soul is gasping for fresh outdoor air.

There's a tired old joke where I live in Southwest Florida, so tired and so old that we feel obligated to keep it on life support: *whether you're going to heaven or hell, you'll go through Atlanta or Charlotte first.* There's one exception: if you're going to South America, you can fly direct from Miami. To get to the Galápagos Islands, whether you come from Miami or Amsterdam, you'll almost certainly pass through Quito or Guayaquil first. Each has advantages. If you choose Quito, you'll probably add at least a day to your trip on each end, which is good if you'd like to visit a big city and get a taste of life and culture high in the Andes. On my first trip, that's what Trevor and I did.

We hired a local guide through the hotel where we stayed for two nights. He drove us to an Andean village and let us drop in on some of his relatives. We saw the guinea pigs that lived around and under their home, including a few roasting on a fire for lunch. We explored a huge open-air market in a nearby town. We stopped at a touristy roadside spot that marked the equator. We hiked around a beautiful lake in the caldera of an extinct volcano.

My two least favorite things about Quito: (1) many restaurants and shops had armed security guards, which always gave me the opposite of a feeling of security, and (2) because I didn't handle Quito's 8,000-foot altitude well, I had some of the worst nightmares of my adult life. But that was just me. If you don't mind (in)security guards and have a good attitude toward altitude, I'd recommend making this stopover. (If you have more time and funds, you might even zip over to Peru and take in Machu Picchu.)

If you stay in Guayaquil, as I did last night, you'll see another modern city, famous, among other things, for huge green iguanas that live in a major city park, wandering around like reptilian pigeons.

In both cities, you can get by without any Spanish, but if you speak even a little Spanish as brazenly as I do, you'll have more fun meeting local people. Last night, of course, I managed to embarrass myself, asking my taxi driver which suitcase (*equipaje* instead of *equipo*) he thought would win the World Cup. In a display of basic human (and Ecuadorian) kindness, he told me he favored any suitcase except Peru. I repeated my embarrassment just an hour ago when I asked someone at the hotel, "Where is the success (*éxito*)?" He directed me to the exit (*salida*) anyway.

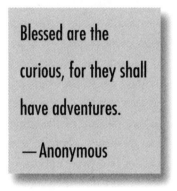

Blessed are the curious, for they shall have adventures.

—Anonymous

As I ponder my superpower of choosing the wrong gender article for Spanish nouns (why is it *el día* and *el problema*?), I wonder how many worse Spanish sins I've committed without realizing it, and how many even greater mercies I've received from gracious Ecuadorians.

Whatever your Spanish proficiency, or lack thereof, if you're an American you might be relieved to know that Ecuador uses American dollars as their currency and requires no special electrical adaptors. What's more, you can find familiar American hotel chains and restaurants in major cities. You may be less glad to discover that the typical hotel cable TV in Ecuador carries Fox News and *The Kardashians*, two things that belong together, I guess, if they belong in Ecuador at all.

Tourists generally visit the Galápagos Islands on guided cruise ships that come in large, medium, or small. My choice for my first visit was a small sixteen-passenger ship, and the fact that I've made the same choice this time suggests that I was amply satisfied. (Land-based tours are also available, and for folks who get seasick, they're the better way to go.)

I suppose if I were an extrovert, I may have preferred a larger ship, but even for an introvert, the experience of sixteen random passengers discovering each other turns out to be one of the greatest things about an adventure like this. Not everyone would choose a vacation that consists of two hikes and two snorkeling trips per day, but in my experience, the kinds of folks who are attracted to this kind of vacation make pleasant and interesting company.

Whatever the size of the vessel you choose, you'll find that the Ecuadorian government takes seriously its stewardship of this World Heritage site. Ecotourism ships minimize the need for tourist infrastructure on the islands themselves, and the government can revoke their licenses if they fail to comply with environmental regulations. Crews of licensed ships understand that their livelihood depends on cooperating with the authorities to preserve this global treasure. They know that 25 percent of its bird species are found nowhere else on earth, along with 27 percent of its mammals, 32 percent of its plants, and 86 percent of its reptiles. In addition, they understand the archipelago's special place in the world of science, both for its historic role in the development of evolutionary theory and for its continuing importance as a uniquely isolated laboratory for ongoing scientific study.

Because they cater to an ecologically sensitive clientele and because their licenses depend on their compliance with environmental regulations, cruise ships tend to minimize waste, use fresh, local ingredients for meals whenever possible, and gently but firmly enforce environmental protections.

If you have a lot of time and you're an experienced (or daring, or naïve) traveler, you could simply land on Baltra

> Everybody needs beauty as well as bread, places to play in and pray in, where Nature may heal and cheer and give strength to body and soul alike.
> —John Muir

(the tiny island whose airport serves nearby Santa Cruz, the central hub of the Galápagos) and then look for last-minute deals on under-booked cruises from the city of Puerto Ayora, the central hub for the whole archipelago. On my first trip, I met some daring folks who toured the Galápagos this way (notably, some young Canadians who could have won gold in an Olympic alcohol consumption event if such an event existed). They hired local guides in Santa Cruz who took them on day trips, and then boarded our ship, which had a few empty beds. They told me they bargained for a really good price. I had neither the time nor the stomach for those kinds of risks.

For most sober people, everything is easier if you work through an ecotravel agency. They have detailed websites that allow you to choose your itineraries, they'll be sure you have the necessary permits, and they know how early you should arrive at airports in Ecuador (earlier than you think because lines can be long and slow).

A Note on the Galápagos Islands

I think you'll enjoy this book if you currently know little to nothing about the Galápagos Islands. The truth is, when I made my first visit in 2001, I didn't even know the islands' names or basic geography. But you'll enjoy this book even more if you have a little basic information.

The Galápagos archipelago consists of five large volcanic islands and scores of smaller ones (over one hundred if you include islets and large rocks that protrude from the sea surface). They are remote, about six hundred nautical miles west of the Ecuador coast. (That's about the distance between Chicago and Washington, DC.) The individual islands were originally named by an English pirate who drew the first maps of the Galápagos. He named them for English naval heroes. You can still find those names on some old maps, but we'll use the modern Spanish names that are now standard.

For the purposes of this book, you really only need to know the names and relative locations of four of the five larger islands.

You can think of these four islands as four letters stretching from west to east (left to right on a map), beginning with a small O, followed by a big backward L, followed by two small Os, one over the other:

The first O and westernmost island is Fernandina. It is the newest island in terms of its volcanic history—after the islands rose from the seafloor in the west, they slowly drifted east on a tectonic plate.

The next island to the east, the big backward L, is Isabela, the largest island, which is really a line of five connected volcanos (the vertical line of the backward L) that bends west to include one more at the bottom (the

horizontal base of the backward *L*). The volcanos from north to south are named Ecuador, Wolf, Darwin, Alcedo, and Sierra Negra (Black Mountain), and then, to the west of Sierra Negra, Cerro Azul (Blue Hill). Between Sierra Negra and Cerro Azul on the south coast is Puerto Villamil, a small port city you'll visit with me later in the trip.

The two *O*s are Santiago to the north and Santa Cruz to the south and slightly east. Santa Cruz is the home of the islands' biggest city, Puerto Ayora, and the tiny airport-island of Baltra lies just to its north, connected by a ferry.

I'm writing this in the Guayaquil airport, which is as modern, over-air-conditioned, and Muzak-infused as any airport in the world. We'll board momentarily and arrive in Baltra in less than two hours, where (my agency promises me) I'll meet someone holding a sign for my ship: *Golondrina*, which means *swallow* (the bird, not the action by which an alcoholic beverage is conveyed from mouth to stomach. And it's *la Golondrina*. I checked).

I try to remain pretty chill when I travel. But I must admit, I really am excited. I'm almost there.

So when does a journey begin?

As I write these words at Gate C14, I know it has already begun.

COMPANIONS

I open my computer at thirty-nine thousand feet. I think about you, the person to and for whom I am writing.

I drift back nearly twenty years in my memory to a large stadium full of people. The lights dimmed. I recall the scent of marijuana, the flash of lighters flickering, the buzz of concertgoers eager for the first song.

Suddenly voices hushed, and a single spotlight illuminated a small circle in the center of a wide, deep stage.

A waifish singer–songwriter emerged from stage right.

She had no backup band. It was just a lone, frail-looking girl in a circle of intense light, her guitar slung on her hip like a machine gun.

She grabbed the microphone in her right hand and touched it to her lips. We could hear her breathe, in and out, in and out, in . . .

She shaded her eyes with her left hand and slowly scanned us, her audience, from her right to her left and back again, from the top high row of the balcony to the

> Now if I hear the sound of the genuine in me, and if you hear the sound of the genuine in you, it is possible for me to go down in me and come up in you. So that when I look at myself through your eyes having made that pilgrimage, I see in me what you see in me and the wall that separates and divides will disappear and we will become one.
>
> — Howard Thurman

bottom front row gazing up at her from below. She was checking us out. Then she uttered one word, followed by one magical sentence.

"Wow," she said in a sultry, breathy voice.

"You're such a great big, strong, handsome, sexy audience."

Then she swung her guitar into place and began to sing.

In that one sentence, the songwriter rendered about two thousand utter strangers into a more manageable single unit. And for the next ninety minutes, she flirted with this composite us, seduced us, and made us fall in love with her through her songs.

She taught me a lesson that night, a lesson in communication that has served me well as a writer and public speaker: a communicator's first job is to make genuine contact with their audience and define their relationship. This memory raises a question for me as I travel from Guayaquil to Baltra, thinking of you. Who are you, my great big, strong, sexy audience?

I imagine you not as an object of flirtation (I'm a happily married man, well over the age of successful flirtation anyway) but as an intimate circle of friends of many ages who fall into two simple categories. Some of you may someday actually take this very flight to Baltra for a once-in-a-lifetime Galápagos adventure of your own. But alas, most of you won't. You have plenty of other things to do and places to see, not to mention other ways to spend a couple thousand dollars.[3]

Although I may entice a minority of you to take this voyage someday, I have another seduction in mind for the majority. If I can breathe these intimate words into your imagination with enough skill and sincerity, I hope I can help you discover and explore not some remote islands in the wide, blue Pacific but the familiar real estate right around you right now—to see wherever you are with fresh eyes, with intensified aliveness, with recharged curiosity and attentiveness.

I dare hope that by imaginatively joining me on this journey, you will come back to wherever you may be, experiencing *right here, right now* in a fresh and enlivened way.

You may be wondering: if I'm such a happily married man, why am I sitting here alone with nobody but you to talk to on this flight to Baltra? The answer: Grace and I are your basic marital cliché about opposites attracting. Grace is a city girl from New Jersey. There are few things less appealing in life to her than snorkeling with sea lions or watching tortoises plod among cactus and thorn scrub. Plus, she gets seasick—even the idea of living aboard ship makes her a little queasy.

---

3. With travel and expenses combined, I kept my total costs in 2018 to $3,400 for eight days. You can very easily spend twice that.

We have many important things in common: values, a taste for science documentaries, enjoyment in binge-watching the same Netflix series (usually), and a shared investment in four amazing kids and five amazing grand-kids. But when it comes to swimming in sometimes chilly and deep seawater, hiking in climates that induce sweat, or getting up close and personal with reptiles, she's like, "Uhhh, no thanks, Brian. Why don't you enjoy this one alone?" (The spouse of a friend says, "If you never leave, how will I miss you?")

So, since Grace didn't come, I'm bringing you with me instead. Which is a good thing for me because the only thing better than doing things you love is sharing those things with people you love. (Wow. Maybe that was a little flirtatious, in a sixty-something, slightly cheesy, authorially distant way.)

I look out my window and see a layer of low clouds hugging the coast of Ecuador. The white blanket extends as far as the eye can see.

Thirty minutes pass and I look down again to see the magic azure of the Pacific glowing where the clouds had been, with the gentle midday blue of the sky meeting the sea at a hazy horizon.

Another thirty minutes pass and the first fragments of the Galápagos come into view. Out of the blue expanse, flat slabs of black and brown rock jut upward, former sea floor, now upraised and carpeted in the gray-beige of sun-scorched grass and desert scrub. Tree cacti dot the land-scape, one here, a few there.

Other distant forms emerge from the sea as well, some of them obviously eroded volcano calderas, others less eas-ily identifiable: rounded mounds or blocks of rock, edged in high vertical cliffs. Off in the distance, the large central island of Santa Cruz slopes gently up toward an ancient volcano, its summit hidden in mist.

Baltra is one of those smaller flat slabs, separated by a thin channel from the northern coast of Santa Cruz. As our plane descends, bumping and sliding in the crosswind, Baltra's landscape reminds me of Arizona or Nevada, except for those unique tree cacti and the vast Pacific Ocean that surrounds it. A faded orange windsock, dancing horizontally, tells me to expect wind as I step out of the plane, but nothing could prepare me for the purity of the air or the perfection of the temperature as my shirt flaps in the breeze.

The air feels alive, almost carbonated.

I have been here for about nine seconds and I'm already in love, in heaven, in ecstasy, as I walk down the stairs to the tarmac.

A covered walkway leads into the large semi-open ter-minal, and a sign above it announces that we are entering the world's only carbon-neutral airport. I take a few steps and realize that the walkway itself is shaded by solar panels. On the other side of the building, I see three massive wind turbines briskly doing their work. Once inside, I notice signs in the bathroom telling me that the dry urinals produce no extra contamination. These innovations are all new since my last visit, hopeful changes that contrast starkly with the grim and regressive fossil foolishness I'm leaving behind in the United States. Don't get me started.

We line up to pass through the islands' special immigration station and pay our $100 Galápagos National Park entry fee. I look at the line. An amazing array of people, mostly young. Lots of well-worn backpacks and scruffy hiking boots adorn travelers for whom the Galápagos is one stop on a larger, longer adventure. I hear Spanish, of course, and German, French, Italian, Dutch, a few different strains of English, some Chinese and Japanese, and a Slavic language I can't identify.

On the other side of immigration control, many folks board a bus that will convey them to a ferry and then another bus to Puerto Ayora, the islands' major city (of twenty-five thousand) on the southern coast of Santa Cruz. It's the travel hub from which many tours depart. Our tour company has positioned two men with a sign to gather sixteen strangers and bring us to our waiting ship in a bay nearby. We begin introducing ourselves.

The first four people I meet are within a decade or so of my age, one from Germany, one from Belgium, and two from England. We are the only travelers over fifty on the trip. The younger travelers are from Switzerland, Germany, Australia, New Zealand, France, and Spain.

We transfer to the *Golondrina* first by a bus to the dock, and then by inflatable dinghy—a bouncy but enjoyable ride to the ship. We make our way to a comfortable wood-paneled dining cabin with padded benches along both sides and four wooden tables that seat four each. We take our seats and look out the surrounding windows: water, birds, cliffs, other ships—splendid views by which to enjoy a late lunch and listen to our initial orientation: safety guidelines, basic schedule, and strong encouragement to follow the strict and wise rules of the national park to avoid damaging what we have come to enjoy.

Our Ecuadorian guide, William, tells us to call him Billy, *Bee-lee,* as he says it. He explains that we're just moving into the season of cooler water, so he recommends we rent wetsuits for our first snorkeling outing after lunch. As we eat, the *Golondrina* motors an hour or so to Mosquera, a small curve of volcanic boulders just north of Baltra into which a rare strip of white-sand beach has nestled itself. After lunch, I rent a wetsuit, goggles, and fins for less than $10 a day and suit up. We take two dinghies to shore, eight passengers each, and have an hour and a half to explore.

We're greeted on the beach by sea lions. I settle down in the sand to watch a juvenile nursing at its mother's abdomen. Mom lies on her back, her flippers akimbo. The juvenile sucks from one nipple, then another, making a kissing sound as it tries all four, and then lets out a goat-like bleat as if to complain that the supply is less than expected. The pup tries again, mom flicking her young one in the face with her rear flipper as if to say, "Mealtime is over, kid." Mom then rolls over on her stomach and the pup joins her in a nap, resting its head on mom's back flippers.

The rhythm of life here has already taken me in. I've slowed down. I have nothing to do besides stay alert for what will present itself to me next.

Nearby on the black volcanic boulders, male lava lizards, each five to seven inches long, are competing for prime real estate. They remind me of playing king of the hill with my pals when we were kids, all of us nearly shivering with excess childhood effervescence. Lava lizards (there are seven similar species spread across the islands) generally have buff-brown bodies with intricate patterns of darker spots and lines, and the males sport red patches on their faces or necks. Where kids on a playground might raise their arms and flex their (mostly imaginary) biceps to show who's king, the male lava lizards do pushups, displaying their red patches like flags, intimidating competitor males and displaying swagger to nearby females.

I walk across the sand and notice the bird-like footprints and tail lines of marine iguanas. I follow the tracks
and see their black silhouettes on some west-facing boulders, well-positioned to catch the afternoon sun after a
few hours of dining on algae in the cool ocean waters.
Across the sand at the high-tide mark are the bleached
bones of a whale, nearly intact, a few displaced, I imagine,
by a sea lion who scrambled through them en route to
the water.

I don my snorkel, mask, and fins and plunge into the water. It's around 70 degrees Fahrenheit—not too cold, but I'm glad for the wetsuit. I feel I'm swimming in a well-stocked aquarium. Along with the smaller green-blue wrasses, black and blue angelfish, beige and yellow butterflyfish, and multicolor damselfish, I see one large parrotfish, impossibly aquamarine and pink, chewing on coral with its formidable beak. A few seconds later, I see a gush of crushed coral stream out of its vent.

Billy later tells us that all of the white sand of that beach came from the digestive system of parrotfish. "Can you imagine the thousands of years of parrotfish pooping?" he asks. "Oh my God!" We learn that this is one of Billy's favorite lines, along with "Look at that! *Amazing!*" "That's a *monster!*" and "That's a $10,000 picture, people! Come on: lights, camera, action!"

He also has a memorable way of referring to a place of abundance as a city: "We're going to marine-iguana city tomorrow." "Look over there: it's tree-cactus city!" "This afternoon we'll snorkel in sea-turtle city."

We return to the ship, shower and dress, and enjoy dinner together. Predictably, I suppose, we've all chosen the same table with the same companions as lunch. Tomorrow, we'll need to mix things up.

I can't help but think of the characters on the old 1960s *Gilligan's Island* sitcom—Gilligan, the Skipper, Ginger,

A human being is a part of the whole, called by us "Universe," a part limited in time and space. Our task must be to free ourselves from this prison by widening our circle of compassion to embrace all living creatures and the whole of nature in its beauty.

—Albert Einstein *(adapted)*

Mary Ann, the Professor, Thurston Howell III, and his wife, Lovey—with whom I spent way too many hours in childhood. I look around and think to myself that as wonderful as the animals of land and sea will be on our voyage, the intrigue of getting to know these companions will be an equal gift. We are sixteen voyagers, thrown together for a once-in-the-universe shared experience, already sharing bread, slowly evolving from complete strangers to a merry band of eco-coadventurers.

RHYTHMS

As we finish dinner, Billy explains that we're already underway, heading north, then west, then south, toward the west side of the largest Galápagos island, Isabela. Our trip will take ten hours, and the sea is a bit rough, he explains, so he encourages us to fall asleep early. "Seasickness will be less of a problem if you are already a-sleeping," he says.

So we all go to our rooms, and I situate myself in my bottom bunk. The sound of the ship's engine and the rhythm of the waves are soothing, and soon I am drifting off into a deep, deep . . . insomnia. But it's about as pleasant an insomnia as you can experience, I suppose.

I find myself remembering the feeling when, as a young boy, well before seat-belt laws, my family would take an annual winter vacation from upstate New York to South Florida. I'd pile pillows and blankets on the floor of the back seat, with my brother stretched out on the seat itself, just above me. We would read and play with toy soldiers as the car rocked in that boat-like rhythm peculiar to cars of the 1950s. Hour by hour, I'd dream of arriving in a warm, sunny place and then of swimming and walking on the beach and maybe finding a crab or sea star. And I would dream of someday visiting the Galápagos Islands.

As dawn fills the room with the shadowless light of a cloudy morning, I realize that I have indeed gotten some sleep, and I'm ready to go for the second day of this voyage of my boyhood dreams.

The daily rhythm begins with breakfast at 7:00 a.m., followed by an excursion at 8:30. Each excursion involves boarding the dinghies, a delicate skill of transferring from one bobbing platform to another. We soon master boat-to-boat transfer with the help of the crew, who teach us not to take their hands but to grasp their forearms, as they do ours. Today we're instructed to board in our wetsuits and with our snorkeling gear in hand, because after touring the coastline for an hour or so, we'll stop in a cove to snorkel.

We're at Punta Vicente Roca, on the northwest corner of Isabela Island. Yesterday's sunny skies gave us emerald-green seas. Under today's gray clouds, the choppy seas vary from grayish green to molten aluminum. A few waves splash over the bow of our inflatable dinghy, but we're dressed for what may come. A young manta ray jumps once, twice, three, and then four times, each time achieving a perfect 360-degree backflip that a snowboarder would envy, his acrobatics serving to dislodge parasites, Billy says. "It looks to me like it's just having fun," one of my shipmates whispers in my ear.

I'm a fisherman, so I suppose my eyes are trained to spot fins cutting the water. I spot one such fin and point it out to Billy. He's ecstatic. "It's a *Mola mola*!" he cries. "It's a *monster*!" Known as the ocean sunfish in English, the Mola

That the day view follows the night view is written large in nature. Indeed, it is one with nature. The next day dawns, the whole heavens are aflame with the glorious brilliance of the sun. This is the way the rhythm moves.

— Howard Thurman *(adapted)*

mola has an improbable shape and a seemingly impossible size. It looks like two giant dinner plates put together, with a huge pair of vertical fins squaring off the back, stretching maybe eight feet from top to bottom.

A few minutes later, I spot another, and soon, a half-dozen Mola mola appear around us. "Change in plans, everyone. This is Mola-mola city! Get on your flippers and masks. Quick! Quick!" Billy instructs. And soon, we're tipping backward off the boat trying to see the Mola mola in all their glory. But alas, they spook, and we return to the boat, only getting a glimpse of gunmetal gray and white in the slightly murky water. We're a bit disappointed not to get a better view but amply invigorated by the cool plunge.

We come to the cove where we'll snorkel in earnest. Blue-footed boobies cling to the cliff—large gull-like birds with legs and feet the color of those latex gloves you typically see in hospitals. Beside them, soot-colored brown noddies roost in crevices, their bills tucked back under a wing. We look up on the top of some nearby rocks, and dozens of marine iguanas sit erect, black as tar, their heads keeping track of us, their tails hanging side by side like locks of a mermaid's long hair. Scattered everywhere are Sally Lightfoot crabs, almost iridescent in their orange intensity. Sea lions with their long necks are ubiquitous in the islands, but fur seals are a rarer sight, distinguishable by necks so short and thick that their heads seem to be installed directly on their shoulders. A family of three fur seals have tucked themselves into adjacent crevices in the cliff. Not far beyond them, a flightless cormorant prunes himself and then suddenly launches into the sea with a lunge not unlike that of a sea lion.

We put on our masks, fins, and snorkels and fall backward again into the sea. The water is a bit murky here as well because of the chop. It takes a few minutes to get comfortable and gauge how close we can safely approach the cliff, rocks, and crashing surf, especially with visibility not more than five or six feet. But it's less dangerous than it looked before we made the plunge, and we gradually stop worrying and start looking for surprises.

I'm swimming along, just barely able to discern the rounded, black volcanic rocks on the sea floor below me, when one of those rocks gracefully ascends to within eighteen inches of my chest: a black sea turtle. She—I know it's a female because of her tiny tail—is obviously resting, not trying to get anywhere, eat anything, or escape from anyone. So I simply stay positioned above her and we float toward shore with a wave and then out with another, again and again, slow dancing in the relaxed tempo of tides. She adjusts her flippers occasionally, keeping herself horizontal. I do the same. She is not afraid of me, not interested in me at all, really. I'm simply a benign part of her environment, and that itself feels like a gift.

> The glory of the Lord is written plainly upon all the fields of every clime, and upon every sky, but here in this place of surpassing glory the Lord has written in capitals. I hope that one day you will see and read with your own eyes.
>
> —John Muir *(adapted)*

How long can this last? I wonder. As long as I want it to, I discover. Slowly we drift apart, but moments later, another black sea turtle, this time a male, rises from invisibility beneath me and for a few minutes, we, too, move together in the rhythm of the sea.

Not long after that a sea lion jets into view and out again, alarming at first because of his speed, size, and unmistakable eye contact. Then a brown pelican plunges in beside me, scooping a pouchfull of minnows. I watch his feet paddle away from beneath the water's surface. Between the rocks beneath me, beautiful reef fish sway in the undulating current, not in a hurry unless I get too close.

I'm having trouble with my mask, so I return to the boat and Billy cleans it with baby shampoo, which not only keeps it clean and defogged but also improves the seal with my face. While he's working on the mask, I float on my back, looking up at the cliffs, following the circling boobies and frigates, the gliding noddies and shearwaters. I feel, amid the constant motion and rhythm of the waves, a perfect stillness. Not the stillness of stasis; the stillness of vital rhythm, the only stillness there can be in this universe of current, spin, and flow.

A little later, back on the *Golondrina* for lunch, I look around at my companions. Each of us has defected from our normal rhythms of waking, showering, commuting, working, commuting, eating, relaxing, sleeping, waking. But perhaps we haven't simply broken out of an old, familiar local rhythm. Perhaps we have temporarily stepped into a larger one: the rhythm of intentional withdrawal or retreat, of vacating old routines to discover a new vantage point through vacation, of recreating ourselves through recreation, of rediscovering what is sacred and of true worth through Sabbath.

I see us as pilgrims, and this Galápagos archipelago is our Canterbury or Lourdes, Mecca or Jerusalem, Santiago de Compostela or Rome.

We are, in fact, worshipers on this boat. We worshiped the Mola mola this morning, and the black sea turtle, the sea lions, and birds, not to mention thirty or more different kinds of reef fish. We worshiped them by determining that they were worthy—worthy of our time, our attention, our

pursuit, our availability. We worshiped them by forgetting ourselves in their presence, humbling ourselves to be benign elements of their environment. We let the reverence and awe they deserved rise within us and wash over us like a wave from mysterious, unseeable depths.

After lunch, I enjoy a siesta.

While the waves rock us in our bunks, Captain Fernando steers south to Fernandina, the westernmost island of the archipelago and the island least affected by humans. It is dominated by a huge, gently sloping volcano that began erupting again just last week. The magma is flowing on the west side of the island, and we're approaching the east side, so we won't be able to see the orange glow, black smoke, or gray steam. But just the same, the knowledge that we're so near an eruption reminds us all of the perilous knife-edge upon which we live.

Even ashore, we are actually floating on a thin, fragile crust, only eighteen miles thick on land, but a mere three miles thick here in the ocean. Beneath that crust, a hot mass of molten rock seethes at 10,800 degrees Fahrenheit, roughly the same temperature as the surface of the sun. Look up, and that blue sky is actually an endless, expanding frigid void with a cosmic background temperature of -455 degrees Fahrenheit. This frigid void is liberally sprinkled with massive, hot, nuclear reactors called stars, each emitting deadly radiation and each ready to suck anything that gets too close into its dense, annihilating furnace. All that protects us from freezing is a thin blanket of atmosphere, which, although technically three hundred miles thick, can only support human life in a 4.5-mile-deep sector.

So here we rock on the *Golondrina*, gently suspended between killer-hot magma beneath us and killer-cold space above us by the thinnest of margins. Think about all this too much and you will bolt up in your bunk in a cold sweat.

We're kindly awakened by the ship's bell for the first of two afternoon excursions, a snorkeling trip in a shallow bay. We don our ritual vestments of bathing suits, wet-suits, fins, masks, and snorkels, board the dinghies, and fall backward into the water, our third baptism of the day.

The water here is clear, and within seconds I see what I most hoped to see on this trip.

A large, black marine iguana is grazing on the lush green carpet of algae that waves and shimmers gently on the black volcanic rocks six feet below me. She is three feet long, chubby, intent on her meal, and utterly oblivious to the wetsuited human being bobbing above her. I start laughing aloud through my snorkel, delighted and grateful.

If you imagine a head of romaine lettuce, and then imagine taking the last half-inch of its leaves, making them so thin they are translucent, and packing them together in patches stuck to the rocks, you'll be able to imagine what her salty submarine salad looks like as she turns her head to one side and then another to clip off a bite. Her line of short dorsal spines marks her as female; a male's would be a bit longer.

Marine iguanas are the only species of lizard in the world to feed under salt water like this—an evolutionary adaptation, biologists surmise, of land iguanas uncounted generations ago when vegetation on land became sparse. You can imagine them first eating the algae available on rocks at low tide, and then, gradually, adapting to dive to depths of several meters.

She seems completely at home in the chilly water, grazing patiently, like an unhurried cow. After a few minutes, she slowly propels herself with her serpentine tail to the surface, just eight inches from my face, takes a breath, and returns to the rocks below. I paddle a little farther and see another, this one a male, and then more and more. When I follow another iguana's ascent to the surface, I notice that she doesn't return to the bottom but starts a meandering swim back to shore. I look above the water's surface and see at least a half-dozen black iguana heads around me doing the same. I realize that their midday rhythm of eating is coming to an end, and they are commuting back to the rocks to restore their preferred body temperature in the late afternoon sun.

I care to live only to entice people to look at Nature's loveliness. Heaven knows that John the Baptist was not more eager to get all his fellow sinners into the Jordan than I to baptize all of mine in the beauty of God's mountains.

—John Muir

As I swim along, plenty more iguanas are still grazing, and there, a black sea turtle is doing the same. Two more sea turtles swim by, not actively feeding but just slowly paddling along. I keep pace with one of them as she moves into deeper water. She comes up within a few feet of me, ascends for a quick breath, then continues swimming slowly beneath me, her front flippers moving in a leisurely tempo, one beat every three or four seconds.

When she descends deeper, I turn back toward the rocky shore and—zip—a torpedo jets by me: a Galápagos penguin. Another and another jet by. I try to keep up but lose sight of them until a minute later when I see them at the surface. Then they dart back down, bending their trajectories in graceful arcs as they chase small fish, bubble trails bending up behind them.

There are still a few iguanas feeding and plenty of turtles to follow, all amid the amazing reef fish that have become expected companions already—angelfish, blennies, wrasses, damselfish.

Occasionally our little group of snorkelers is joined by some young sea lions who make the rounds among us like jubilant puppies. One makes an impossible turn and comes nose to nose with me, his huge eyes meeting mine through the glass of my mask. We share a brief moment of mutual recognition, and then in a flick of his fins he is gone to frolic among other swimmers. The young pups, I later learn, are mischievous and playful, often toying with marine iguanas, sometimes to lethal effect for the iguanas.

Fortunately for the iguanas, the pups outgrow this playful and sometimes destructive stage by the age of five months. Then they get on with the more serious behavior of sea-lion adulthood. But even then, that playful streak is never fully gone.

Our snorkeling excursion ends. Back aboard the dinghies, we are as jubilant as sea lion pups, each bubbling over with stories of encounters. Companions with underwater cameras share their photos and footage as we ride back to the *Golondrina*. After showers and a snack, we board the dinghies again and make a dry landing (from dinghy to rocky shore) to trek the volcanic landscape we viewed earlier from the water. We pass several "iguana cities" and a few "iguana metropolises," where the coal-black reptiles are resting in huge aggregations, utterly unworried by our presence.

Suddenly, several dozen iguanas rouse and scatter in all directions, from lethargy to agility in an instant. A Galápagos hawk, the main predator of young iguanas, has flown in and tried to snatch a juvenile. The hawk missed but continues to sit among the larger lizards, who for a few minutes seem wary, but soon return to their default Zen-like calm.

We walk on the lava rock, just below a dune of gritty sand. In that sand, Billy explains, iguana eggs are incubating. A few minutes later, one of our number spots two newly hatched iguanas in a crevice in the rocks. "They hide there because they would be a perfect snack for that hawk," Billy says. "It's not safe for them to bask in the open until they're bigger."

> What is going on? We are returning to the homeland of our birth. We were lost among machines, shut up in offices with air-conditioning and dried flowers, absorbed in myriads of talking pictures. Now we are returning to the vast planetary and cosmic community.
>
> —Leonardo Boff *(adapted)*

On our way back to the dinghies, we walk among sleeping sea lions scattered near the water's edge. Some groan and moan in their sleep. Some snore. All remain oblivious to our presence. Billy explains that when males reach sexual maturity, they can become aggressive rather than playful. In fact, during breeding season in December, we wouldn't swim here because alpha males would see us as intruders. "Our sharks are very, very friendly. We have never had one single record of a shark attack in the Galápagos," he says. "But every year, many alpha male sea lions injure people who fail to show them proper respect." Sounds familiar among humans, I think to myself.

At dinner, I shift to a different table and meet some new people. Most of the folks on a smaller yacht like this are budget-conscious, and many are serious travelers with lots of adventures to share. Everyone's comparing notes, asking what's best to see in Peru or Chile or Afghanistan. Those who have visited the United States are amazed at its natural beauty but communicate a polite yet firm distaste for the bitter turn our politics has taken—a distaste I share, I assure them.

We sleep at anchor, but at about 4:00 a.m., the engines roar and we head south and east across the channel that separates Fernandina and Isabela.

When I wake and climb to the upper deck, the sun is rising over Urbina Bay on the west coast of central Isabela. The coastal foothills of Volcan Alcedo wear a mantle of verdant green.

A new day, a new rhythm.

CONTRASTS

Our second day brought me the gift I was most hoping for, marine iguanas feeding underwater. This third morning brings a gift I haven't dared hope for.

We make a wet landing (from dinghy to surf to sand) in bare feet in Urbina Bay. On the gritty black-sand shore, we put on our shoes for a walk through the green scrub forest that covers the foothills of Volcan Alcedo. The rim of the volcano is always verdant, but the coastland here in this region is dry and scrubby from November through May. On a June morning like this, you would never guess that. The dry thorn bushes of winter are sprouting with leaves, and birds are everywhere—finches, doves, mockingbirds, warblers.

Billy leads us inland on a well-worn path. He points out some large turds composed of partially digested fibrous grasses. "That's a sure sign," he says. "The tortoises are here." We notice tracks in the sand: four toenails dragged between footprints. We turn a corner and there

they are, their wrinkly gray necks outstretched in the morning sun. One, two, three large ones, probably one hundred to three hundred pounds, and a so-called small one, maybe sixty pounds. "Oh my God!" Billy says, his trademark sign to us that we should be excited. Seeing one is good, two is great, but four together? An "Oh my God! Tortoise city!" bonanza!

Our little group huddles, takes pictures, then settles into an observant silence. The largest tortoise walks toward a bush, bends down her neck, and delicately lifts a few small fruits from the ground, each slightly larger than a grape—manzanillas, they're called. Billy tells us they're poisonous to humans, but the tortoises love them. (Their common name in Spanish, *la manzanilla de la muerte*, literally means "the little apple of death.") Each year after mating in December and January near Alcedo's rim, the tortoises begin their slow trudge downward. It takes them three months, eating as they go, to arrive here at the coastline where they lay their eggs and enjoy a few months of lowland living before plodding back up to the Alcedo highlands in August or September.

Like so many of the other creatures here, they pay us no mind. One walks in our direction, not to greet us, but simply because he wants to get to some point beyond us. We move aside, and he passes. Farther up the trail we pass another, and later, we will encounter three more, including a male slowly following a female, romance on his mind, but she gives him the cold shell shoulder.

Now I realize why we saw no tortoises in the wild on my first trip to Galápagos in January of 2001. They were all in the highlands, and we only stayed near the shore. To see eight in one morning seems, how shall I say it, "Oh my God! Amazing!"

The guides here have learned not to rush, to let people take their pictures, ask their questions, simply soak in the experience. "It's okay to take a few minutes to meditate," Billy says. I think his word choice is perfect.

As we pause among tortoises in the shade of some trees, the tortoises browsing on abundant fallen manzanillas, Billy tells us the history of the tortoises. Before humans arrived in the sixteenth century, scientists estimate there were half a million tortoises spread across the archipelago. By the middle of the twentieth century, the number had shrunk to twenty thousand. Of the fifteen or sixteen varieties, four went extinct, and all but two varieties are still considered vulnerable.

What happened to the tortoises is what happened to so many species, too many species, during the era of the conquistadors. And of course, the conquistador spirit lives on today, as does the carnage. I stand in the shade and can't help but wonder: How many so-called real-estate developers, protected by their bought-and-paid-for politicians, will send armies of bulldozers to conquer and destroy in hours what it took millions of years for sun, wind, earth, sea, and our fellow creatures to develop? How many acres will be un-developed? Who will even notice?

Any fool can destroy trees. It took more than three thousand years to make some of the trees in these Western woods — trees that are still standing in perfect strength and beauty, waving and singing in the mighty forests of the Sierra. Through all the wonderful, eventful centuries since Christ's time — and long before that — God has cared for these trees, saved them from drought, disease, avalanches, and a thousand straining, leveling tempests and floods; but God cannot save them from fools — only Uncle Sam can do that.

—John Muir *(adapted)*

For modern-day conquistadors, the long-term health of natural ecosystems never gets a second thought. Short-term profit is always their first, last, and only concern.

Between the sixteenth and twentieth centuries, tens of thousands of tortoises were hauled by conquistadors and their descendants onto ships and tipped on their backs. Even in this condition they could stay alive for a year with no food or water, so they became like free meat that didn't need refrigeration. I try to imagine them stacked in ships' holds, slowly starving, with nothing to look forward to but more suffering, a hatchet, and a cooking pot.

Meanwhile, careless humans turned domesticated animals loose on the islands. Some, like goats and pigs, were released intentionally, so the sailors could return later and catch a fresh supply of meat that had multiplied on its own. Others, like rats and dogs, were released unintentionally and went feral. The results were the same: The goats multiplied and decimated the land of vegetation, leaving tortoises to starve. The pigs ate everything in sight, and quickly learned to dig up tortoise eggs as a protein-rich snack. Hungry rats and dogs sniffed out and consumed baby tortoises and any other living thing.

Like indigenous people facing invading hordes of colonizers armed with guns, cannons, smallpox, and theologically infused arrogance, the indigenous tortoises didn't stand a chance against these feral invaders, whether human or nonhuman.

Billy then turns to the story of the Darwin Research Station and the valiant attempts of conservationists "doing their best" (Billy's repeated phrase) to help the tortoises recover from the worst done by their fellow human beings. He includes the famous story of the tortise called Lonesome George, the last surviving

member of the Pinta Island gene pool. After decades of best attempts, researchers could find no mate for George. Billy recounts the moment when he was visiting his family on the mainland and heard about George's death on TV. "He was so young when he died, maybe just seventy," Billy remembers sadly.

That is young indeed, considering a baby tortoise taken from the islands by Charles Darwin himself in 1835 lived for 172 years, dying just a few years before Lonesome George.

As Billy shares his stories, flocks of Darwin's famous finches drop to forage for seeds in the sand. Mockingbirds, yellow warblers, and other birds I don't recognize call from the trees around us.

We walk a little farther and come upon the first of several land iguanas, descendants with the marine iguana of a common ancestor. A bit bigger than the largest marine iguana, the land iguanas in this region of Isabela are a brilliant yellow. They let us walk past with all the apprehension of a lazy dog resting on a sun-drenched rug.

We return to the beach with a half-hour to ourselves. One of my companions goes snorkeling and calls to me from the water, telling me I made a big mistake leaving my gear on the *Golondrina*. This lagoon is full of sea turtles, sharks, rays, and other sea life, she says. But I am happy to bask on the sand, feeling a bit reptilian, watching the world from a tortoise's unhurried perspective.

A pelican dives, a penguin bobs up and as quickly disappears, and a dark oval rolls through an aquamarine wave—a sea turtle just below the surface. A while later, a fin appears in the surf at the water's edge, then two. Two small sharks swimming in formation? No, a young eagle ray, its spotted wingtips piercing into my fragile world of air and wind before the wave in which it rides recedes.

Years, seasons, moon phases, tides, waves rolling in rhythm on the shore with unexpected gifts.

We return to the ship and motor north along the west coast of Isabela, enjoying lunch and a siesta as we go. By midafternoon, we're anchored in Tagus Cove, notable because visitors to the cove painted graffiti on its rocks for decades, if not centuries, until the National Park restricted access to travelers unaccompanied by a trained guide. The graffiti, as unfitting as it is to the natural setting, functions as a reminder of the same sad, stupid human capacity for carelessness that resulted in the deaths of hundreds of thousands of tortoises and so much other devastation. (I wonder as I scan the graffiti if my whole state of Florida, or what remains of it after sea-level rise, will one day be viewed by future humans as one stupid, shrinking crime scene of careless graffiti.)

An apt Wendell Berry quote comes to mind, about there being no such thing as sacred and secular places, but rather sacred and desecrated places. The slaughter of

By far the most remarkable feature in the natural history of this archipelago is that the different islands to a considerable extent are inhabited by a different set of beings. I never dreamed that islands, about fifty or sixty miles apart, and most of them in sight of each other, formed of precisely the same rocks, placed under a quite similar climate, rising to a nearly equal height, would have been differently tenanted.

—Charles Darwin *(adapted)*

tortoises, like paint slapped on rocks by vandals, was an act of desecration and natural sacrilege. In contrast, the saving love-labors of scientists and activists to protect, reproduce, repatriate, and restore stand out as holy acts of reconsecration, returning vandalized ecosystems to their original sacred status.

We pass among the graffiti-painted rocks and hike up into the steep foothills of Darwin Volcano. It's arid here and there is little green to be seen. The crunch of our footsteps on the gravelly path fades quickly into an eerie silence. One of our group christens the area a ghost forest, an apt name for the stand of mature palo santo trees that cover the hillside as far as we can see. Their naked bark shines gray-white in the austere sunlight, each trunk and branch stark, erect, without a single leaf or bud. Billy explains to us that in November and December, rains come here, the trees leaf out, and the air is full of the songs of finches who nest in their branches. But by June, all the leaves have fallen and there is hardly a bird to be seen. We're less than thirty miles from Urbina Bay, but the combination of geography, prevailing winds, and ocean currents renders this nearby microhabitat vastly different.

The trees get their name because of their fragrance. Catholic priests burned them to make incense, hence the Spanish name "holy sticks." Holy sticks, unholy slaughter, pathetic graffiti—so many contrasts.

We're hot when we return, so we quickly prepare for a snorkeling trip, this one along another cliff face.

Above the surface we see layer upon layer of brown-gray rock, representing millennia of volcanic ash deposits. Below the surface, our familiar reef fish defend their little sacred home territories. King angelfish truly are regal, larger than a man's hand, with a white slash cutting across their blue-black body, their fins bright yellow to burnt orange, edged in neon blue. Around them swim butterflyfish and damselfish of many kinds, along with blennies, gobies, and wrasses that hide in the rocks, painted with a rainbow of neon blues and yellows, velvet blacks and reds, subtle browns and beiges. Schools of larger fish swim by in the deeper water, yellow-tailed mullet and yellow-tailed surgeonfish resembling a shimmering armada of waving flags as they pass.

In almost every cove we find sea turtles, this one wedged in among rocks, asleep; that one eating algae from a submerged cliff wall; several slowly passing by in no hurry to arrive anywhere. I've seen enough turtles now that I begin to notice smaller features, some shared by all, like vestigial claws on their front and back flippers, others unique to each turtle: barnacles on a right front flipper; a heavy growth of green algae carpeting a carapace; a white spot, probably a scar, above an eye; a bite-shaped notch in a rear flipper, probably inflicted by a male trying to dislodge a rival mounted upon a female during mating.

This world is marked, I think as I swim along, marked by beauty and violence, marked by the rapacious ignorance of some and by the holy resilience of others doing their best to restore what has been desecrated.

We return to the boat and eat our dinner early. We have already begun our long journey of ten or twelve hours to retrace our voyage of day one, rounding the north end

of Isabela and returning to the vicinity of Santa Cruz, the central island. Our chef, Victoriano, has prepared a delicious dinner, but one by one or two by two, all but four of my companions leave the galley. The sea has grown rougher, and the early effects of seasickness have drained them of their appetites. For some reason, my stomach is spared, and I hardly notice the rocking and rolling of the waves. If anything, I enjoy it.

After the meal, I join my fellow sailors, those who aren't in bed, on the upper deck. There's a strong wind and the moon is bright. To our right we see the north end of Isabela bathed in silver light, volcanos Ecuador and Wolf silhouetted black against the moonlit sky. Then we round the point and Isabela is still on our right, even though we're sailing due south now. I chart my course to bed and sleep well to the roar of the engine and the roll of the waves.

When I awaken at dawn, all is still.

PEACE

The main engines are off, and even though the ship's generator is still humming beneath my cabin, the ship feels calm.

I dress and ascend to the upper deck and realize that we are on the lee side of a new island, so the seas are barely dimpled.

I take in the relative silence: the sound of light wind in my ears, now-dry bathing suits gently flapping like flags, pinned to a line strung from the ship's rigging. Occasionally a sea lion complains from shore with a pathetic bleat.

I can barely make him out, an elongated brown potato lying inert on the coal-black sand of low tide. Around the ship I hear small splashes, the sound of fish feeding on the surface. I look down and see the unlikely source of the sound: brown and tan pufferfish. I've seen them often as they slowly glide through the water while I'm snorkeling; I didn't know they could move so fast when feeding on minnows at the surface. On shore to my right, I hear the golondrinas, our ship's namesake, voicing the familiar twitter of swallows around the world.

The word *twitter* reminds me that I haven't used or even thought about social media for—how many days now? I've lost track. Could it be Monday already, the halfway point of our trip? Social media, days and dates, current events—they've all been totally forgotten, rendered nonexistent, less than irrelevant here. I can't remember the last time I went four days without any social-media activity or curiosity about the doings of politicians whose names I'd rather not even mention.

I've been so immersed in this actual reality, these actual moments and these actual places, that I've forgotten that such a thing as mediated reality even exists.

Come to think of it, I haven't looked in a mirror in four days either. How long has it been since I haven't spent even one thought on how I look?

I am taken back to an almost-forgotten memory from 2005, when I began visiting slums around the world as preparation for a book on global crises (including extreme poverty and the slummification of humanity). I was in a poor barrio whose name I can't remember, somewhere in Central America. As I walked among the shacks and shanties, I noticed how many had TVs. In a few, I saw kids playing first-generation video games like Pong and Tetris; in others, *Walker, Texas Ranger* strode in to save the day the proud American way, with guns, fists, and excessive confidence.

My memory then fast-forwards to another shantytown in 2006, this one in South Africa, and this time, I can see satellite dishes rigged on the roofs of many homes, with electric lines sagging from house to house. Dirt roads, skinny dogs and trash everywhere, massive unemployment—and these people have cable TV, I think to myself. I walk among the homes, and there's Chuck Norris again, spreading the swaggering gospel of Texas to South African slum-dwellers.

That scene ended up in a spoken-word song I wrote called "11:57," which I start chanting to myself:

We made a suicidal system, and we said it was predestined. We said devil made us do it. We told a lot of lies. It was a system of injustice, built on

Our consumer culture defines the "abundant life" as one in which "natural resources" are sacrificed for human profit and pleasure and "human resources" are the employees who will work for the lowest wages. Both nature and poor people are means to the end of consumerism.

—Sallie McFague

arrogance and greed. It was an empire for the powerful, and a hell for those in need. A suicidal system. A suicidal system.

We made a suicidal system, and we turned a handsome profit, and we made a billion guns and more wars to utilize them. And we keep the poor in slums, to ignore them or despise them, and we broadcast shows and movies, to amuse and tranquilize them . . . in the suicidal system, the suicidal system.

We made a suicidal system, and we pumped it full of toxin, and we killed off lots of species, and we made the world an oven. And we built a lot of churches, and we saved a lot of souls, but we destroyed a lot of good things, and our way of life was full of holes. A suicidal system. It's a suicidal system.

We made a suicidal system that cannot be sustained. It must be redirected, and we must be retrained, to reclaim our true identity in harmony and care, with saving love for everyone to free all creatures everywhere from the suicidal system. The suicidal system.

We made a suicidal system, and we pray it's not too late, but it's 11:57, so we'd best not hesitate. It's time for a defection, to choose a new direction, to seek for reconnection, pass through death to resurrection from the suicidal system. . . . The suicidal system.

There is another system, another way to go. It's nearer than the air you breathe. It's better than you know. It's a sacred ecosystem. It's invisible but there. It's a gentle revolution; it's the answer to our prayer, an answer to our prayer.[4]

---

4. The song is available to listen to and download on my Bandcamp page: https://tinyurl.com/y58v2jd3.

I don't like disturbing the peace of this morning with thoughts like these, but for a few moments, I can't help it. Isn't the alternative digital reality of TV and social media, to some degree at least, the perfect strategy of an exploitive, destructive economy, keeping us distracted in a digital world while its elite gangs of robber barons steal, kill, and destroy the natural world? I think of C. S. Lewis's classic *The Screwtape Letters*, and I imagine a slobbering senior demon of unrestrained capitalism giving a speech to his underling devils:

> If we keep them busy with *Walker, Texas Ranger* reruns and Twitter, if we worry them constantly about how they look in comparison to others, they won't notice while we slaughter the tortoises, toxify the oceans, and turn ten thousand forest paradises into ten million parking spaces. Ha! We'll be filthy rich, and those fools won't even notice!

I shake off all those dark thoughts and return to this bright morning, this cleansing morning breeze, which I notice is picking up now.

The clouds directly above me are turning yellow, colored by a sun I can't yet see, hidden by a bank of clouds that covers the volcano summit near the center of the island in front of me. The daily morning mist that moistens the higher elevations here nearly every day has a special name:

garúa. I've only read about it, never felt it, since access to the interior is so limited for sea voyagers. But I imagine it to be like the mist I've experienced in a thick mountain fog back in North America.

> Once more, we need to reject a magical conception of the market, which would suggest that problems can be solved simply by an increase in the profits of companies or individuals. Is it realistic to hope that those who are obsessed with maximizing profits will stop to reflect on the environmental damage which they will leave behind for future generations? Biodiversity is considered at most a deposit of economic resources available for exploitation, with no serious thought for the real value of things, their significance for persons and cultures, or the concerns and needs of the poor.
>
> —Pope Francis *(adapted)*

The high yellow clouds soon turn white, and the sun sets the top of the lower cloud bank afire. It's about to break through.

To my surprise, though, the winds delay the sun's coming into view by carrying that low cloud over our bay, and suddenly I feel garúa on my skin for the first time, lighter than rain but heavier than mist, refreshing and sweet.

The cloud passes and full morning breaks just as the breakfast bell rings. After a breakfast of fresh fruit and French toast, we board our dinghies and soon wade through the gin-clear water to the black-sand beach of James Bay, along the west coast of Santiago Island. The bay is known to the locals as Puerto Egas, named after a scurrilous character whose story Billy shares with us on the beach.

Victor Egas was from Guayaquil and visited Santiago in the 1920s. He discovered salt deposits about a forty-five-minute walk up the volcano's slope. Egas knew there was a market for salt on the mainland, so he hatched a plan. After buying a huge tract of land and building a house for himself on the bay, he returned to the mainland. Egas started telling people a tall tale: Arid, thorny Santiago was a paradise, he said. Just walk in from the shore and you'll find avocado, banana, and papaya trees galore. The land is fertile, and you can each create your own farm. He convinced several dozen impressionable mainlanders to join him. When they arrived, they quickly discovered the truth about dry Santiago, and about deceitful Egas himself.

Once on the island, the people had no way of escape, and Egas quickly reduced them to something close to slaves. At night they slept in a crude dormitory, the ruins of which we can see just above the beach. From dawn until dusk they were forced to haul thousands of buckets of salt to the coast, and along with the salt, they carried thousands of volcanic boulders so that Egas could build a jetty from which the salt could be loaded into ships.

Egas planned to build a whole city to indulge his fantasy of riches. But to fulfill his dream, he needed more money, so he traveled back to the mainland to request a huge loan from a Guayaquil bank. He persuaded them, as con artists have a knack for doing.

When he returned to Santiago, nobody knows what happened for sure, but things didn't go according to his plan. Some say Egas's slaves did him in. Others say he fled to Brazil or Argentina to avoid having to repay the bank's money. Whatever happened, the bank repossessed the land and, decades later, donated it to the national park. The ruins of a house, dormitory, and water tank now stand as a memorial to this dark episode in the history of the Galápagos.

Even if Egas had succeeded, his city would have been short-lived. He was building on volcanic ash, also known as tuff, and even now, less than a century later, the ocean is reclaiming the land he thought he had claimed for himself. He was a clever fool and a confident fool, but a fool nonetheless.

Stories like this, of course, have occurred the world over because clever fools can show up anywhere and find people to seduce with their confidence, which, by the way, is the source of the terms *con man* and *con artist*. The poor fools who have been fooled by a more clever fool are all too ready to cover up the story to save face, which explains why Puerto Egas was renamed James Bay, a respectable name to conceal a dark story. Behind how many concealments do the slobbering demons of consumptive capitalism still count their mounting profits, keeping their kleptocracy a delicious secret?

We walk to the far side of the bay where lava rock spills out into the sea. The black rocks are dotted with radiant orange Sally Lightfoot crabs, the only real scavengers of the archipelago. Sunbathing tourists who fall asleep on a beach have awakened to find themselves surrounded by Sally Lightfoots, who think their next meal has washed ashore.

I hear a familiar sound, the song of a yellow warbler, common throughout North America from Alaska

and Nunavut south through Mexico to northern South America. Through most of their range, yellow warblers are more often heard than seen because they're secretive, preferring to hide and sing from the high, leafy branches of trees. Here, though, the yellow warblers show both themselves and their adaptivity, hunting for insects along the lava rocks of the shore. They've certainly lost their timidity here. Several hop within an arm's reach of us as we sit or stroll among the tide pools, behaving more like English sparrows in a city park than any wild warbler I've ever seen.

Billy leads us at a leisurely pace, leaving us free to notice what we will. That's at the heart of the job of a good guide, I think: to set a pace where those in his charge will be likely to notice things we wouldn't have noticed otherwise, and then to be present for our questions.

We return to the beach and put on our snorkeling gear. This is the clearest water of our trip, and I realize I've forgotten to bring my flippers. I decide to turn my mistake into an opportunity: I'll snorkel alone, not trying to keep up with others, and will proceed at the pace my arms take me.

I enjoy the patterns of sunlight dappling the tar-black volcanic sand one, two, even three yards down. Schools of silver-gray mullet come and go above the rippled bottom. I reach the ruins of Egas's stone jetty, now submerged by ninety years of wave action. Thousands of oblong stones, each taking a portion of an involuntary worker's day and strength to carry, sprawl out across the sea floor, looking like the graveyard where irregularly shaped bowling balls go to die.

Now, these underwater monuments to human folly and cruelty are being reclaimed by sea life. Slate-pencil sea urchins dot the stones, each looking like a small, jet-black tomato into which short blue-gray crayons have been stuck. Fish swim among the boulders as if human folly had constructed a fish condominium especially for them.

Just before I head to shore, I see something ahead in the shallows that becomes the highlight of the morning and one of the highlights of my trip. It's a sea turtle, but unlike all of the gray-black specimens I've seen so far, this one is intensely hued, its dazzling colors impossible to fully capture in words, especially as they shimmer under a foot or two of crystal-clear seawater.

It is not enough, however, to think of different species merely as potential "resources" to be exploited, while overlooking the fact that they have value in themselves. Each year sees the disappearance of thousands of plant and animal species which we will never know, which our children will never see, because they have been lost forever.

—Pope Francis

The skin of her head is banana yellow, and each scale on her head is a rich copper brown. The same color scheme applies to her front flippers. On her back flippers, the scales meet, so no yellow is visible. The turtle slowly drifts toward me, and I change course, positioning myself thirty inches above her.

I use my arms when she uses her front flippers, and we slowly move in formation out to the depths. For a while, the black sand of the bottom is visible, and her bright yellow head and limbs almost glow in shimmering contrast. Then the bottom drops away, and I find myself staring at the marbled beauty of her upper shell. The base color is hard to name, but gray-green comes close, maybe dark olive. I see flecks of orange and even purple against that base color, patches of a brighter green fading into browns, with subtle highlights of beige and gold.

She is unbothered by my presence, and slowly she ascends until she hovers between ten and twenty inches from my mask. We cruise along like this for maybe one hundred yards. The sun casts bright, undulating arcs of concentrated light on her carapace, and I yield to the temptation to reach out and gently run my fingers across her smooth shell, the only park rule I've knowingly broken. She shows no reaction, but continues to paddle, glide, paddle, glide, and so do I, in a long, gentle arc.

I realize that I've followed her back to the rock-pile jetty ruins where the water is less than three feet deep. I decide to let her swim on alone, grateful for fifteen minutes spent in her company. In two or three strokes of her orange-brown flippers, she is over the top of Victor Egas's cruel folly, and I make my way back to shore, feeling like a pilgrim who has kissed an icon.

A gift, for free. No advertising, no con artistry, no quid pro quo, no fooling, just a graceful animal and an honest, respectful encounter, priceless moments of beauty and grace.

• • •

We return to the *Golondrina*, and as we eat lunch, we cruise for about two hours to a stopover at Chinese Hat, a small island that we visit by dinghy. The beach is made of pieces of bleached white coral, most of them about the size of a grape. Billy explains that every time there is an El Niño climate pattern, the water warms up so that coral can grow quickly. Then, when El Niño passes, most of the coral dies and is washed up on beaches like this one, if it isn't chomped on by parrotfish first and transformed into excreted sand.

Billy uses our stroll around Chinese Hat as an opportunity to teach us the basics of volcanism. So much of our planet is formed by volcanoes, I think as he speaks, that every earthling really should know this as part of our basic planetary lore. When tar-black magma emerges from the earth, it is heavy and hot, well over 1,500 degrees Fahrenheit. As it cools, it often hardens into odd shapes, elongated globs resembling a stack of ropes, for example. This kind of lava is called pahoehoe, a Hawaiian term pronounced *paw-hoey-hoey*.

When magma is less hot as it is ejected from the earth, it cools and hardens quickly, and the iron within it also oxidizes rapidly, often giving it a reddish or brownish color. This type is called aa, pronounced *ah-ah*.

> The universe unfolds in God, who fills it completely. Hence, there is a mystical meaning to be found in a leaf, in a mountain trail, in a dewdrop, in a poor person's face. The ideal is not only to pass from the exterior to the interior to discover the action of God in the soul, but also to discover God in all things.
>
> —Pope Francis

When surface magma cools and hardens while the hotter subsurface magma continues to flow, lava tubes and tunnels of various sizes form, some a few inches in diameter, and others, several feet.

On this side of Chinese Hat, the volcano spewed the cooler aa type of magma, so the area resembles a huge mound of brown Swiss cheese, full of tunnels. When parts of the tunnel walls crack or collapse, little caves form. In one such cave, about the size of a refrigerator, we see a sea lion resting, comfortably sheltered from the midday sun.

During some eruptions, magma explodes out as fine dust or grit called ash, and when the ash falls, it creates huge flat expanses, some many meters thick. At their edges, these ash fields often show clear layering, resembling sedimentary rock you might see in nonvolcanic regions.

Black pahoehoe lava, brown aa lava, and ash—they tell the geologic story of Galápagos for those with eyes to see.

Our lava lesson complete, we return to the ship and prepare for a late-afternoon snorkel along a stretch of Santiago Island, just across a narrow channel from Chinese Hat. This coastline is black pahoehoe magma from a relatively recent eruption, geologically speaking, about 130 years ago. We swim just a few meters from the sharp rocks, as waves break not far to our left.

I'm amazed at how different the fauna is here. Yes, many of our old favorites are still present: king angelfish, yellow-tailed surgeonfish, sergeant majors, blue-chin parrotfish. But we see many new species as well: impressive schools of small reddish-orange fish we haven't seen elsewhere, each maybe two inches long and glowing as if they carry embers in their copper-colored bellies. Later in the *Golondrina*'s library I'll learn their name: pink cardinalfish.

Schools of black-striped salema swim nearby as well, less careful to stay near the shelter of the rocks. They're silver with black horizontal stripes, and when a large school surrounds me, I feel I'm in a shimmering blizzard of tinfoil confetti.

Along with the slate-pencil sea urchins, there are light green sea urchins scattered among the rocks and sand, and I spot one larger buff-colored specimen with crew-cut spines less than a half-inch long: the white sea urchin or sea egg. I also see my first sea cucumber, a gray-white elongated blob in a patch of sand. I've heard that they used to be common, but that their stocks have been depleted by local fishermen eager to satisfy Japanese and Chinese seafood markets. A whitetip reef shark swims out from under a ledge of rock. It's maybe three feet long. It circles and then returns under its ledge. I hear some nearby snorkelers shrieking excitedly through their snorkels, feeling a thrill of danger, even though the danger is imaginary.

What delights me most in this unique microhabitat are the sea stars. On previous dives, I've seen several

many-legged sea stars similar in shape to a sunflower, but chocolate brown with bright orange dots: the sunflower star. Here, I see a much larger star with similar coloring, but of a more conventional five-pointed shape: the Panamic cushion star. They're scattered generously on the sandy bottom in deeper water. In one area, several sea stars of another species cling to the black rocks with long, thin arms, their mottled olive-gray color giving the pyramid sea star its ghost-like appearance. I notice one species of star that is so rounded that its five points are barely visible,

Have we really won if we achieve a rapid rise in GDP at the cost of decimating the environment, dropping more and more families below the poverty line, and neglecting education, culture, and quality of life?

—Philip Clayton

the aptly named chocolate chip sea star. It's cookie beige with raised and rounded brown-to-black spikes.

Back aboard the *Golondrina*, as day passes into dusk, I realize that I'm now past the halfway point of my trip. So often, the second half of anything good seems to pass more quickly than the first half, from the second half of a pizza to the second half of a great book. I wonder if that will be the case this week.

Then I remind myself that if I'm not in too great a hurry, if I don't run from this adventure to the next too quickly, if I discipline myself to reflect, savor my memories, review my photographs, reread these words in my journal, just as it is hard to say when a journey begins, it will be hard to say when it ends.

But if I fall back into the suicidal system, if I believe the lies of Victor Egas in his many current incarnations and play the fool to those slobbering, scurrilous demons of consumptive capitalism, my journey will have ended before I cross the threshold of my home.

After dinner, I climb back to the upper deck to end the day where it began for me. I see one of the *Golondrina*'s crew has his cell phone out. We're near enough to Santa Cruz that there's a signal, he says.

Is this a temptation I will resist?

SIGHT

I didn't resist the temptation last night.

Before going to bed, I texted my wife from my phone, just to let her know I was okay and to be sure she was too, nothing more. My son Trevor, who had accompanied me to the Galápagos Islands seventeen years earlier, is visiting her. Here's our exchange:

> Me: Hi! I'm doing great. Having an amazing time. You okay? I will have spotty cell coverage at roaming rates until tomorrow, then back off grid.

Just want to say hi and I love you! Hi to Trevor too—so many photos to share!

Grace: [no answer]

This morning I wake early. We arrived overnight in Puerto Ayora, the most populous town of the archipelago, so I go to the ship's upper deck with my phone and computer, hoping to hear from Grace and then do some writing.

There is a strong signal here, but still no reply from my wife.

I scroll through my photos and pick a selfie of me standing near a giant tortoise from Urbina Bay, and I send that to her, hoping it will nudge her to reply to my message from last night. Apparently last night's message never went through, but this one does. Immediately. Go figure. Within seconds I hear the *bing* of an incoming message.

Grace: Great to hear from you. Are you okay?

Me: Doing great. All is well. Love and miss you!

That's it.

Then, like an addict returning to his crack pipe, I completely fold in my resolve to stay unplugged and try to get online with my phone. I manage to check a few emails before the signal fails. I try to connect again. I check the news and learn the latest depressing shenanigans of my government and its president, and again the signal fails.

At this point, I feel that the universe is conspiring against my social-media relapse, so I give up, turn off roaming on my phone, and decide to do some writing on my computer.

There is only one problem.

It's dead. Like, scarily nonresponsive, even-though-it-had-been-charging-all-night dead. I try everything I can think of short of whacking it on a table. Still nothing. I feel haunted by the 12,591 words I have already written of this book but not yet backed up—potentially lost forever in melted-down circuits within my MacBook Air.

So I do what any desperate, computer-dependent writer would do.

No, I don't pray.

I turn my phone's roaming function back on and franticly text my wife again.

I ask her to ask our son Trevor what to do, knowing that Trevor, being a millennial and therefore automatically a computer genius, will know or quickly find the answer.

But I get no reply. Of course.

Soundly defeated on all technological fronts, with no access to virtual-mediated-digital-artificial-augmented reality, I have to settle for the actual unmediated reality visible not through an Apple screen but courtesy of the dawn light over Puerto Ayora.

My bleary eyes look up from my keyboards and screens, blinking like a man not-quite-yet miraculously healed from blindness. I take a deep breath and survey the bay that surrounds me.

The sky is cloudy, although I can't tell if it's morning fog that will burn off or a more lasting, all-day gray. (It turns out to be the latter. In fact, it turns out to be a long-term, rest-of-the-week gray.) I look down over the railing

> All you have to do today is go outside and gaze at one leaf, long and lovingly, until you know, really know, that this leaf is a participation in the eternal being of God. It's enough to create ecstasy.
>
> — Richard Rohr

beside me and see about ten small sharks circling our boat, more than I have seen in all my snorkeling so far. They are blacktips, as gray as the sky, with touches of black right where you'd expect, given their name.

The bay is dotted with boats and ringed with buildings, most of which have a 1960s feel: square contour, square windows, painted white or gray, squarely functional. The considerable charm of the town is not evident at all to this technologically defeated traveler trying to get unstuck from the gray moment.

I recognize the dock area from my earlier visit, and then I remember that there are several big statues of animals along the waterfront, a little amateurish and gaudy, as I recall. But I can't remember exactly what they are statues of. A tortoise? A crab? A fish? I'll see soon enough, because we will be disembarking for town after breakfast.

Just then, a black Darwin's finch joins me, seeking crumbs in the blue outdoor carpet. "Consider the birds of the air," he seems to be saying. "They neither tweet online nor check their email, but they find all the crumbs they need." I barely have ears to hear, much less eyes to find crumbs. I scan the shore, my mind on other things. Is there a computer repair shop in Puerto Ayora? I wonder.

On either side of the town, the coastline is arid, brown-gray, a few tree cacti jutting up from the scrub. East of the town, looking to my right from where we are anchored, the volcano slopes up, up, up into the clouds.

Victoriano opens the galley window below me and throws some kitchen scraps into the water. A school of pufferfish quickly gathers, fighting over them. Soon one of the blacktips returns, veering into the pufferfish repeatedly and only narrowly missing getting one for breakfast.

The bell rings, signaling it is time for ours.

Immediately after a breakfast of fruit, cheese, bread, and a perfectly fried egg, we will begin our excursion in Puerto Ayora, so I quickly go to the youngest member of the crew, Robert. (I am making a logical inference from an uncontested law of physics: *a person of advanced age tends to remain computer incompetent, unless acted upon by a younger and superior force.*)

I show him the tragic dark screen of my computer. "No funciona," I say. "¿Cree usted que hay alguien en Puerto Ayora que puede arreglarlo?"

"Dámelo," he says confidently. "Tengo un amigo." I give him the computer, and he puts it in a plastic bag and stows it in a small backpack. He cancels whatever plans he has for the day—his only free afternoon in his hometown—and joins us on the dinghy to town. He leaves us at the dock, and the last I see of him, he's jogging up the street, the backpack bouncing on his back.

While Robert is busy trying to save my career as a writer and make the sentence you're now reading possible, I visit the Charles Darwin Research Center in Puerto Ayora with my fellow travelers.

Six of our original group had signed up for a five-day cruise only, and this is the day they depart and six new travelers join us for three more days: one from Austria, two from Switzerland, two from the United States, and one from Spain. We meet our new companions at the dock and walk toward the Center together.

We stop at the fish market on the waterfront. It's full of the expected sights—and smells—with the added sound of sea lions persistently begging for scraps: *uuuuah! uuuuah! uuuuah!* Pelicans wobble around as well, more somber mendicants, arguing for a scrap based on a body language of sympathy rather than volume: *Don't I look pathetic?*

Don't you want to feed me? The staff goes about their business, stepping over and around sea lions and ignoring pelicans at every turn.

We reach the Center and pause near the entrance for a history lesson from Billy.

For millions of years, the Galápagos Islands were untouched by humans, he explains. Then, when humans invented transoceanic sailing vessels, a succession of explorers, conquistadors, and pirates stopped by to find fresh water and fresh meat. After an English explorer drew the first rough maps of the islands in 1684, the archipelago was known as the Enchanted Isles, in large part, I imagine,

I was baptized in balmy sunshine that penetrated to my very soul, warming all the faculties of spirit, as well as the joints and marrow of the body; in the mysterious rays of beauty that emanate from plant corollas; and in the spray of the lower Yosemite Falls. Consequently all Baptists are my brethren, and all will allow that I've "got religion."

—John Muir *(adapted)*

because explorers felt the native animals were under a spell. "Normal" wild animals, the Europeans knew, were afraid of people. But these animals showed no fear.

The human response to the friendliness of the animals was predictable: they slaughtered them, especially tortoises. Tortoise meat fed sailors at sea; tortoise oil lit homes on the mainland. Populations of tortoises plummeted, along with iguanas, sea lions, and birds (many, like flamingos, taken only for their feathers or else as substitutes for Christmas turkey).

In 1832, Ecuador claimed the islands and decided to make the small southern island of Floreana a penal colony for its worst offenders. The prisoners suffered harsh treatment at the hands of their jailers and in turn inflicted harsh treatment on the innocent fauna.

Prisoners, sailors, pirates, and early settlers alike shared a common superstition: if you drink the blood of a tortoise, you will gain its longevity and you'll extend your—let's say male potency. Soon, the bleached shells of slaughtered tortoises littered the landscape, victims of two perennial human obsessions: beating death and erectile dysfunction.

Floreana was the site of the first tortoise extinction.

Meanwhile, feral animals, introduced by pirates and adventurers, were spreading through the islands, multiplying human devastation indirectly. Decimated by humans and outcompeted by feral animals, three more varieties of tortoise went extinct, reducing the number of varieties from fifteen to eleven. And eventually the number dropped to ten, because the Pinta population went extinct with Lonesome George in 2012.

Starting in 1934, laws were passed to protect parts of the islands. But 1959–60 marked the real turning point for the preservation of the archipelago's creatures. First, all uninhabited parts of the islands were declared nature preserves. Second, the Charles Darwin Foundation was formed in Brussels. Third, the Charles Darwin Research Station (CDRS) was built here in Puerto Ayora on Santa Cruz Island. Some years later, the Galápagos National Park Service (SPNG) was created and its headquarters were built right next to CDRS.

The interrelated work of SPNG and CDRS has grown, so that now there are over two hundred park rangers working with SPNG and over twenty researchers working at CDRS to protect the Galápagos ecosystems. In addition, the tourism companies hire guides like Billy, who, with researchers and rangers, share a commitment to protecting the islands. For many years, the guides were nearly all foreigners, but in recent years, highly trained Ecuadorian guides have become the norm, many of them born and raised in the islands.

Because of the work of the Park Service and CDRS, rapid destruction of the islands has been slowed almost everywhere. In some places, destruction has been halted, and in many places, reversed. The eighty-four tourist vessels licensed to host visitors to the islands must work under Park Service supervision, and the CDRS has become a must-see attraction for nearly all visitors. With some notable exceptions, more and more local people have learned to take pride in their island paradise and share with CDRS and SPNG a commitment to preserve it.

The researchers and park rangers have indeed done amazing work over these last six decades. They began with the massive task of eliminating tens of thousands of feral animals. They located and transported the most endangered populations of tortoises and other species to CDRS so they could be protected, studied, and then bred for eventual reintroduction. Meanwhile, new threats have arisen, such as an invasive fly whose larvae feed on native bird chicks, a plant parasite called the cottony cushion scale that destroys many native plants, the blackberry bush that spreads rapidly and harms both native forests and agricultural areas, and, of course, a warming global climate and rising sea levels, which will likely prove the most dangerous threat of all.

Billy finishes his talk, and we wait in a short line to see a little monument to Lonesome George, his body carefully preserved through taxidermy, enshrined in a glass case in a small building. A sign says not to stay more than six minutes in the building. I am happy to leave after less than one, eager to see the living tortoises that are signs of hope and life rather than this reminder of human plunder.

As our little group walks together down the trail and into the breeding facility, we first come to some naturalistic enclosures with large adult tortoises. They have ponds to soak in, big rocks to climb over for exercise, and plenty of room for either solitude or interaction, whatever they prefer.

In contrast to the stuffed remains of poor old Lonesome George, many of the living tortoises on display represent welcome stories of unexpected success.

For example, Billy had told us that the Floreana population of tortoises was the first to go extinct. That was true, in the sense that there were no tortoises left on Floreana. But some years ago, researchers found a group of about seventy tortoises on the Wolf Volcano of Isabela that seemed different from the neighboring Isabela populations. DNA tests were conducted, and the CDRS staff discovered that these were actually transplanted Floreana tortoises. Nobody knows how, why, or when, but at some point, a group of Floreana tortoises were dropped off on Isabela, and enough survived to sustain a population of seventy.

Several were brought to Santa Cruz to be part of a breeding program, and they're on display at the Center now. Over 120 eggs have already hatched from this group,

and these young tortoises will soon be repatriated to their original home on Floreana. That means that the number of extinct species has dropped from five to four, and the number of extant species has risen from ten to eleven. Measurable progress!

There is virtually no hope that any other species will be recovered in this way.[5] But some of the most highly threatened populations are making a heartening comeback.

---

5. Surprisingly, while this book was in production, one lone survivor of the Fernandina population, thought to be extinct

We come upon one such group of resilient animals in the next enclosure. These are tortoises from Espaniola. Their population was decimated because of an infestation of goats that consumed all the vegetation, robbing the tortoises of both food and protection from the fierce equatorial sun. Only two males and two females remained alive, and they were brought to CDRS for protection.

Word went out to zoos around the world to see if any zoos had additional Espaniola tortoises. In 1976, the San Diego Zoo responded. They had one male. They sent him to CDRS, where he was named Diegito (Little Diego) in the zoo's honor. Diegito has turned out to be a super-successful sire. The CDRS colony, with their star stud Diegito, has produced so many fertile eggs over the last several decades that now over a thousand young have been repatriated to Espaniola. Many of these captive-born young have already reached sexual maturity and are reproducing so successfully in the wild that CDRS has discontinued the breeding program. More progress!

---

for over one hundred years, was discovered and brought to the Research Station. There is hope that other individuals will be found to join this female so a breeding program can begin. "Virtually no hope" is not "no hope"! See Alex Stambaugh, "'Extinct' Galápagos Tortoise Found after 100 Years," CNN, February 21, 2019, https://tinyurl.com/y4oz7tlq.

As we watch the tortoises resting, eating, soaking in the ponds, and slowly climbing and descending the rocky areas of their enclosures, we hear a strange sound, something between a cow mooing and an old man groaning. We follow our ears to a huge male from the Floreana group. He is mounting a female in one of the ponds, uttering a mating grunt or groan, the only vocalization tortoises ever make other than a hiss when they pull into their shells. Because tortoises are deaf, the mating grunt has no effect on the female.

> It was less like seeing than like being for the first time seen, knocked breathless by a powerful glance.
>
> —Annie Dillard

We go over and observe the process, awkward at best. A few minutes later, we hear a similar sound from the Espaniola group. Even though it isn't breeding season, nobody has informed these males. They are clearly staying in shape.

Next, we come to the rearing pens for juveniles. The smallest babies, those under a year old, are kept in covered pens for protection from rats, which readily kill and eat newly hatched tortoise babies. Each pen contains a cohort of tortoises of the same birth year and variety. After the juveniles reach roughly the size of a cantaloupe, they're transferred to larger uncovered enclosures with more natural topography to navigate, which prepares them for release into the wild when they're four or five years old. Then their shells and skin are thick enough that they are no longer at risk for predation.

CDRS is both sobering and inspiring. After we view all the displays, we make our way back through town toward the dock. Along the way, I see two things that can only be seen in the Galápagos Islands: first, a sign that says ¡CONDUZCA CON PRECAUCIÓN. CRUCE DE IGUANITAS. CUÍDALAS! (*Drive with caution. Baby iguana crossing. Take care!*), and second, a sidewalk littered not with newspapers and beer cans but with basking marine iguanas.

I have maybe twenty minutes to spare, so you can guess what I do.

I find a coffee shop that advertises Wi-Fi, buy a cup of something as an excuse to get the password, and check the messages on my cell phone. The message my son had sent hours ago finally arrived:

Shut down the computer completely. Plug in your AC adapter and make sure it's delivering power. Using the built-in keyboard, press and hold the

Left Shift, Command, Option, and Power buttons at the same time. Release all the keys at the
same time. Press the power button to power on
your computer.

Well, I think, maybe that would have worked. But I'll
never know. We'll see if Robert is having any luck when
we return to the boat for lunch.

But Robert isn't there. He hasn't missed a single meal
before this, and I am a little worried. Has my data, including this manuscript, joined four tortoise varieties in the
zone of eternal extinction?

I will have to wait until dinner to find out.

After lunch, we go back to town and board a bus for a
trip to the highlands. In my 2001 trip, the highlands were
not part of our itinerary, so I am excited to see the homes
and farmlands of the local people, and especially the ranch
that is our destination.

As our bus makes the gentle ascent out of town, we
see obvious signs of Puerto Ayora's growth. *Se Vende* and
Privada signs sprout everywhere. Aside from the little
paved highway we travel, the side streets are red dirt, lined
with small homes and buildings in various stages of con-
struction. Eventually we enter farming territory, full of
mango and avocado trees, banana groves, and gardens visible from the road.

Soon we are in ranching territory with cattle grazing in the lush green foliage and barbed wire stretching between trees and fenceposts, many of which sprouted branches once they were placed, a phenomenon I have witnessed in fertile areas from Southeast Asia to East Africa to Central America.

Three or four miles farther, we turn left onto a dirt road. By now, the garúa of the highlands has intensified into a light rain. We take this road for another few miles, passing lots of cattle along the way. The bus slows and everyone starts laughing. I look from the back of the bus between heads and see through the windshield a large tortoise crossing the road to (ahem) get to the other side—in his own sweet time, of course. From this point on, we see a tortoise every thirty seconds, this one grazing among the cattle, that one munching grass at the side of the road, another one stretching his neck to bite a leaf in the rich strips of forest between ranches.

When we reach Rancho Manzanillo, those careless travelers who forgot to bring raincoats (including me) are able to buy cheap plastic ponchos in the ranch's little store, trash bags with hoods really, of translucent pastel pink or blue. We don rubber boots provided by the ranch (gumshoes for our Australians), and Billy leads us on a tour of the ranch, telling its story as we go.

Every hot season (November and December), Santa Cruz's tortoise population concentrates here in the highlands where it's always moist and green. During these months, the slow, low grunting sound of mating echoes through the forest from dawn to dusk. Then, beginning in February and March, the tortoises slowly migrate back down the slope of the volcano toward the coastland in a three-month trek, eating all the way. The females nest in June and July. By August or September, they begin their upward migration again, returning to the highlands to mate again in December.

This idea of migrating tortoises strikes me as odd. Migrating birds, monarch butterflies, whales, caribou, and salmon? Sure. But tortoises? I can't imagine it. Why migrate, I wonder, especially when life would be good for them if they stayed here in the highlands all year long? I try to imagine some evolutionary mechanism that would wire migration into the tiny brain of a tortoise, motivating it to plod six or seven miles down a slope of 1,200 feet and then, a few months later, trudge back up again. A person might make that trek in three hours, but what would keep a tortoise going in something close to a straight line for three months? And if they were moving that slowly, how would they remember where they were going—or why?

And then the irony hits me. Just a few hours earlier I was frantic to check my email and panicked about my computer. For the previous four days, I had so enjoyed slowing down my pace, syncing up with more natural rhythms: sunrise, sunset, wave, tide. But then, enticed by a lousy cell-phone signal, I had so quickly jumped out of that rhythm, back into the civilized rat race that zips around at the speed of light rather than plodding, tortoise-like, at the unhurried speed of life. I can't decide whether to scold myself, laugh at myself, pity myself, or simply allow myself to rest back into a rhythm and pace modeled more on a migrating tortoise and less on an urban rush hour.

While I am deep in my own thoughts, Billy has begun the story of how this land became a tortoise sanctuary.

In 1961, Hermain Guerrero Solis and his wife, Rosita Villalva, arrived in the Galápagos Islands from mainland Ecuador. They worked hard as farmhands for a few years, saved judiciously, and bought the ranch, where they planted gourmet coffee. They always appreciated the tortoises and decided to dedicate part of their land to their protection. Eventually they developed the ranch for ecotourism, allowing people to walk among wild tortoises and see upland forest flora and fauna up close. They began working closely with CDRS and opened their doors as Rancho Manzanillo Tortoise Preserve in 2012.

Billy explains that several other ranchers in the area have gotten in on the ecotourism market, some more for profit than preservation: "I know another rancher nearby here. He has cattle and pigs. He used to hate the tortoises because they would plow through his fences when they migrated in and out of the area. He would sometimes kill the tortoises by flipping them on their backs, and once he was convicted of poisoning a watering hole to kill them. He got in a lot of trouble for this. Now he has opened an ecotourism preserve like this one. He charges each visitor five dollars, and he might get 150 visitors a day. But I prefer to bring my guests here to Manzanillo Ranch because these people truly love the tortoises. I would rather good

> The seeming value or dignity of an object doesn't matter; it is the dignity of your relationship to the thing that matters. For a true contemplative, a gratuitously falling leaf will awaken awe and wonder just as much as a golden tabernacle in a cathedral.
> —Richard Rohr

people like them get the entry fee, and then you can buy some food or drink or souvenirs at their little shop to support them also."

One of my German companions asks Billy, "If the tortoises migrate away during the cooler months, why would people keep coming to the ranch when the tortoises are gone, and why are there still tortoises here now?"

"These are very good questions. Germany should be proud of you," Billy replies. "Most of the large tortoises have already departed. Each day, a few more will leave. Later in July, all of the big ones will be gone. But remember I told you that the ranch cooperates with CDRS? The Station now has a place to send young tortoises that they have hatched and grown to a reasonable size. These tortoises are maybe only ten or fifteen years old. Until they reach sexual maturity at twenty or twenty-five, they do not migrate. So this gives the CDRS a place to return young tortoises to the wild, it gives the tourists a chance to see animals in a natural setting year-round, and it gives the young tortoises a safe and natural place to grow."

We walk the grounds in our pastel ponchos, encountering a few large tortoises and many younger ones along the trail. We can stop and observe them as long as we want, along with the abundant bird and plant life, including verdant lichen- and fern-covered trees and plenty of manzanilla trees with their small yellow fruit. Billy reminds us not to eat these "little apples of death" because of their toxicity to humans.

When we return to Puerto Ayora, we have some time to walk the waterfront before the dinghies arrive. I find those statues I remembered from seventeen years earlier. They are indeed a little gaudy, somewhere between kitschy and cheesy and maybe even creepy: an albatross, a tortoise, a fisherman, and a land iguana.

Back on the *Golondrina*, it is time for dinner. Robert is busy setting the tables. When he sees me, he quickly exits the dining room and disappears down to the lower deck.

A few minutes later he returns. He presents my computer to me, completely fixed. The receipt says the cost was thirty dollars, paid from Robert's pocket. I take out my wallet, reimburse him, and tip him another thirty dollars.

I'm thinking of increasing the tip tomorrow.

Theologians and philosophers often speak of classical arguments for the existence of God: the ontological, cosmological, and teleological arguments, for example, or the argument from design, beauty, or consciousness. Whenever I'm prone to doubt the existence of a kind and benevolent God—or a kind and benevolent human, for that matter—I hope I'll recall "the argument from Robert."

And then I can add the argument from Hermain Guerrero Solis and Rosita Villalva, and the argument from CDRS, and the argument from hundreds of thousands of tourists who pledge each year to join in the work of protection and conservation.

There's lots of ugliness to see in the world and in people. But there's goodness and beauty too—so much goodness and so much beauty. Saviors of many kinds abound, if we have eyes to see.

But of course, unless we slow down enough to notice, we might as well be blind.

ICONOGRAPHY

We awaken on day six of our journey in Puerto Villamil on the south end of Isabela, having motored west for about sixty miles from Santa Cruz as we slept. From the upper deck of the *Golondrina*, I see the lights of the small town reflecting orange and yellow on the mirror-smooth water. There's almost no wind this morning in this protected cove. Above, a low ceiling of gray clouds hovers just over the rooftops. We board the dinghies for a before-breakfast walk on a nearby island just off the coast. When we disembark, we pass a covered porch with benches for people awaiting transport. A large sea lion has claimed one of the benches. He belches out a bark at anyone who comes too close. This is *his* bench, thank you very much, and he has no plans to share it.

We walk along a trail and enter a lava field that feels as unearthly as any place we've seen. Vertically angled chunks of black rock have eroded into knife-sharp edges, making the area impassable if not for our narrow trail. Most of the rocks are topped in a chalky white substance—patches of lichen, smooth as primer paint. In some places, more typical green-gray lichens grow on the black rock surface as well.

Lichens are among the first living things to colonize volcanic rock, Billy explains. We see little else alive here until we come near the water's edge and find marine iguanas arranging themselves with their backs pointing east to capture the meager radiant energy coming through the morning clouds.

In a gravelly patch between the sharp rocks, a rare lava gull, large and drab gray, pokes among some white scraps. Billy tells us that the scraps are sea lion vomit. Among the scales and bones that the sea lions can't digest, the gulls find morsels of nourishment.

I wander around taking pictures, drawn in by the black-and-white landscape of this volcanic island. A marine iguana's scaly black leg, foot, and toes extend stark as coal against satiny white lichen. Two iguanas sit nose to nose, silhouetted and still against the silver-gray waves that slowly undulate beyond them. Nearby, a male iguana's spiky crest runs like a fence of bleached pickets down the center of his pebbly head and neck. Below the crest, each scale of his body stands as distinct as a black cut diamond, and below his body, the lichen spreads, as if an eggshell melted, then froze. I try to catch this visual poetry with my camera, but it defies the capacities of lenses and pixels, just as it defies the capacities of words.

As we return to meet our dinghies for transport back to the *Golondrina*, my right ankle brushes against one of the lava boulders. As I sit in the dinghy, I notice a line of red blood running into my shoe. And that from just a light touch!

After breakfast, we board the dinghies once again and head to Puerto Villamil for snorkeling. There's a lagoon at the edge of town that Billy wants us to experience. When we arrive, a ranger tells us that the lagoon has been closed to tour boats like ours. It has been too crowded, so now it's only open to day-trip tourists. A few among us grumble, suspecting this has more to do with Puerto Villamil trying to entice extra business from the day-trip boat operators.

We make plans to go to another cove, but the ranger tells us that is not allowed either, and then relents, allowing us entrance to the original place. Twenty minutes wasted, but then again, in those twenty minutes we've observed how bureaucracy survives and evolves even in the Galápagos.

The lagoon proves to be worth the wait. It gives us our first and only opportunity to snorkel among mangroves, waxy-leaved trees that stand on stilt-like roots in salt water. Although many of our familiar creatures are here, we discover plenty that are new.

Once I'm in my wetsuit, I climb down to the water's edge and launch myself. There's an initial rush of cold, but the wetsuit does its job and I feel comfortable within ten seconds.

The water is clear, and I immediately notice thousands of brown sea anemones carpeting the rocks here, their tiny circles of upraised tentacles poised to seize any passing shrimp or similar tiny morsel. Just yesterday, I remarked to myself that I had seen very few anemones, which surprised me. This cove more than makes up for the earlier deficit.

Out in the deeper water among the black volcanic rocks, familiar reef fish dart in and out of holes and crevices. Yellowtail damselfish are especially common here, as are cigar-shaped Cortez rainbow wrasses, but with a difference.

The Cortez rainbow wrasse comes in distinct color phases according to its sex and maturity. On small fish, horizontal stripes run from nose to tail: yellow, maroon, red, and hot pink. As they grow, both males and females become even more beautiful. Their foreheads sport a round patch of brilliant electric blue. Their backs

> God is not out there or back there or yet to be, but hidden in the most ordinary things of our ordinary lives.
>
> —Sallie McFague

are an iridescent maroon with deep blue to olive green undertones. Across their midsection, a single narrow stripe of vibrant banana yellow runs horizontally the length of their body, and beneath the stripe, the belly is silver-white to light blue. Beneath the body, the ventral fin is edged with a radiant blue or hot purple-pink. I'm tempted to echo Billy's "Oh my God! Amazing!" whenever I see one.

Up until now, we've only seen these baby and juvenile color phases. But here in this lagoon, another phase is also present in a few of the largest individuals. The horizontal markings are completely gone. The whole head is now an electric azure blue. The horizontal yellow stripe has been replaced by a wide vertical yellow band behind the gills, and the rear half of the body is a violet-fuchsia, culminating in a brilliant azure tail.

Each stage is beautiful, and if I hadn't consulted a book in the *Golondrina* library, I would have assumed each was a distinct species. To add to the complexity, I later learned why the rare phase is indeed so rare relative to the others. On occasion, a female turns into a special male called a *terminal male*, which guards a large harem of females. If the terminal male dies or leaves, another of the females will become a terminal male, gradually assuming his distinct coloration. This gender fluidity, it turns out, is surprisingly common among fish, shrimp, worms, lizards, and some other creatures, and it helps explain why distant evolutionary descendants like us have complex sexual identities that often defy the simple binaries of male and female.[6]

I venture out in the deeper water and see a monstrous ray resting on the bottom, roundish in body and a dark gray in color. It appears to be well over three feet in diameter. I assume it's a torpedo ray, although later, when I consult the *Golondrina* library, I read that they aren't supposed to get that large. Later, I'll do some more research and conclude it was a marble ray, notable for being unafraid of divers and also willing to defend itself with its potent stinger.

A companion swims up and points to a mangrove tunnel from which she just exited. I enter through a crack between black volcanic rocks. Mangrove branches arch over my head and roots descend on either side, fringed with tiny shrimp. When I exit the mangrove tunnel, I come upon a large sea turtle feeding in less than two feet of water.

She isn't highly colorful like the turtle I swam with yesterday, but neither is she the monotone charcoal black of the turtles we swam with on the northwest coast of Isabela. She's halfway between. Her carapace reminds me

---

6. For more on the fascinating subject of gender fluidity, listen to Molly Webster, "Gonads: X & Y," *Radiolab* (podcast), New York Public Radio, June 30, 2018, https://tinyurl.com/y6oumh4q.

of a granite countertop, mottled black, gray, brown, and tan, merging in a beautiful pattern. The mottled pattern continues on her head and front flippers. Because the water is so shallow and she is so intent on feeding, I hover beside her, her face and my mask eye-to-eye. I am close enough to watch her chomp on a clump of algae and chew on it a few times, each time using her tongue to compress it against the roof of her mouth so that sand and silt trapped in the algae are expelled in a cloud through her nostrils.

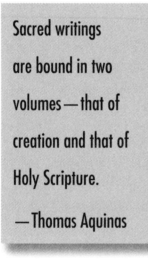

Sacred writings are bound in two volumes—that of creation and that of Holy Scripture.

—Thomas Aquinas

Each time she pulls away a clump of algae, a terminal male Cortez rainbow wrasse darts in to catch any shrimp or other small creatures that are dislodged in the process. I watch her eat for maybe ten or twelve minutes, both of us bobbing to the rhythm of gentle waves, and as she moves from rock to rock, a new terminal male Cortez rainbow wrasse darts in to get a snack. The dominant wrasses clearly have established a symbiotic relationship with the turtles. The arrival of a turtle must be to them like the arrival of an ice-cream truck was to me as a kid.

We come to the edge of the rocky area where the turtle has been feeding, and then she begins swimming across the cove. The floor descends, and now I am swimming about thirty inches above her, a perfect vantage point to enjoy the dappled pattern on her carapace. The rear-right quadrant of her shell is scarred by four huge gashes. Could it have been a shark, I wonder, or a sea lion? No, the spacing between the scars isn't right. Then the obvious answer dawns on me: these are propeller marks. I've seen identical marks on manatees back home in Florida. Scars like these are an occupational hazard of living near humans, even here.

I arrive back at the starting point, haul myself out, and gather with my companions, all of us bubbling over with stories of what we've seen in this magical mangrove cove.

We return to the boat for lunch and then come back to Puerto Villamil for an outing a few miles inland. We walk a few blocks from the dock to a large flatbed truck to which has been added a wooden cab with six rows of wide benches, not exactly a bus, not exactly a truck, but a transitional evolutionary form. The bus takes us up a red-gravel road to a large artificial lagoon, the result, Billy explains, of a recent gravel-mining operation. The bottom of the large mining pit has filled with a foot or so of water, and flamingos have discovered it and made it a favorite feeding and resting spot.

We see two groups of pink-orange flamingos standing in its shallow muddy water. The far group looks like seven balls of cotton candy, each balanced on a thin stick. This is how they sleep: one foot extended, the other folded against the body, with head and neck tucked under a wing. The closer group of four are feeding, but their actions seem so synchronized that it feels right to describe what they're doing as a feeding dance.

When one dips its head in the water, all the others do too, moving their beaks slowly back and forth in the mud, filtering for organic material and small shrimp as they go. When one takes a step forward, so do the rest. And when one raises its head to rest and look around, they all follow suit. Their thick, down-curved bills are yellow tipped in black. We watch the dance for several minutes, snapping pictures that we know won't do justice to the elegant flamingo choreography we've witnessed.

We walk down the road to another tortoise breeding center. Many years ago, researchers at the Santa Cruz facility discovered that relocating eggs over long distances by boat seriously reduced the successful development of the embryos, so the Arnaldo Tupiza Chamaidan Giant Tortoise Breeding Center was established in 1994 here on the south end of the largest island, Isabela. This facility specializes in breeding and rearing species from this island only.

We pass through a modest educational exhibit and then encounter a herd of tortoises from a unique and recently discovered population.

On the slopes of the Cerro Azul Volcano to the northwest of Puerto Villamil, there is an area called Five Hills. A small population of adult tortoises was discovered there. They were considered part of the larger Sierra Negra population in southern Isabela Island, but these tortoises differed in shape both from their Sierra Negra neighbors and from any other group of tortoises on the islands.

Some tortoise shells, like the ones we saw near Volcan Alcedo a few days ago and the ones we visited yesterday on the ranch in Santa Cruz, are highly domed. Others have an upturned front that resembles a saddle.[7] Still other tortoise shells are intermediate between the two, somewhat domed and slightly saddlebacked.

The Five Hills tortoises resembled the intermediate variant, except that their shells looked like they had been

---

7. Tourists are commonly told that the old Spanish word for *saddle* was *galápago*, which gave first the tortoises and then the islands their names. That etymology may be mistaken; see Christopher Klassen, "Galápago or Galápagos? The Origin of the Name behind the Enchanted Isles," Santa Cruz II blog, March 7, 2018, https://tinyurl.com/y3ompugp.

squashed down in the center. This flattened Five Hills population was few in number to begin with, but when the Cerro Azul volcano erupted in 1998, extinction seemed imminent. Scientists rushed in to rescue eighteen adults, and they are the tortoises who greet you in the first large corral when you arrive. Several were burned by volcanic ash, and the scars are still visible on their shells twenty years later. Fortunately, they've adjusted to captivity well, and they've turned out to be very fertile too, producing over two hundred babies for repatriation.

A little farther along the trail, we come to another group of tortoises that were even closer to extinction than the Five Hills group. People hunted this group so

> God's boundless compassion, especially in its many and varied ecological expressions, embraces all of us in the warm heart of nature's church, calling to us to worship therein, and to protect this worldwide green temple as our loving home and common destiny.
>
> —Mark Wallace

relentlessly that researchers were only able to locate eight survivors: four males and four females. They were brought to the breeding center and they also have proven fertile.

As at CDRS, babies of each group are kept in covered cages for protection from rats, which have proven impossible to eliminate completely from the archipelago. (Lava rock with all its crevices and tunnels is basically the perfect rat habitat—"Rat city," as Billy says.) And also as at CDRS, larger and less vulnerable juvenile tortoises, those over a year or two old, live in uncovered corrals where they can wander and forage in preparation for repatriation.

Our group wanders (but doesn't forage) slowly from corral to corral, observing at a slow pace these creatures that live at such a slow pace.

We pass a bulletin board with charts displaying the breeding success for these and other groups of tortoises at the Center. Over 3,000 hatchlings have led to over 2,300 repatriations, leaving just over 700 tortoises currently growing at the Center.

We wander back to the town along a boardwalk through mangrove lagoons. We see some more flamingos, along with common stilts, black and white as if tuxedo-clad, with impossibly long and thin black bills and even more impossibly long and thin bright blood-orange legs. Billy tells us that their local nickname is "Italian Gentleman," and I can immediately picture a black-and-white film from the 1930s or '40s, with elegant Italian men at a dinner party smoking cigarettes in long cigarette holders.

We have two hours of free time in Puerto Villamil. I wander the beach with some companions and eventually settle down alone at a beachfront bar with a Wi-Fi signal. I order a pilsner, munch some popcorn, video-chat with my wife and son, thank them for their help with my computer coma the day before, catch them up on the happy ending to the story, and then they catch me up on news of the family. Unlike yesterday, today my use of technology feels purposeful, intentional, relational, not driven by techno-addiction or one of my spiritual nemeses: FOMO, the fear of missing out.

But ironically, while I am virtually "with" my wife and son at the bar, I am actually missing out on something that's happening just a few blocks away.

I hear about it as soon as I'm back aboard the *Golon-drina*. A few of my shipmates ask to sit with me at dinner. They know from previous conversations about my spiritual and professional background and the writing project that brings me on this adventure, and they are eager to share photographs of something they experienced together in Puerto Villamil.

Their wanderings took them to Cristo Salvador Catholic Church. The doors were open, so they went inside and took photographs especially with me in mind.

To my eyes, the outside of the building in the photographs looks a bit odd, but perhaps *unconventional* would be a kinder term. Its exterior is white-painted cement, stuccoed with a wavy pattern, and each wall is scalloped on its upper edge, perhaps to evoke waves on the sea. A pointed white cement arch draws attention to the main entrance with its bold red door. Inside, the building has a modern feel, unostentatious, with cement floors, simple wooden benches, a metal roof, and unconventional angles.

In the apse of the church, a dramatic life-sized statue of Christ is suspended halfway to the ceiling on the front wall. This is no typical crucifix with a dying Jesus, evoking sympathy and maybe a little guilt. No, this risen Jesus is young and muscular, his arms outstretched and reaching forward, scarred on his wrists and feet, but utterly, vibrantly

> One has a sense of belonging to the earth, having a place in it along with all other creatures, and loving it more than one ever thought possible.
>
> —Sallie McFague

alive. No halo surrounds him or marks him as separate from the local environment. He exists fully within it, a vital part of it.

Behind this robust figure is painted a scene unlike any I have ever seen in a church. There are no heavenly thrones or angels in this painting, no golden streets or harps. Every element of the mural's imagery is earthy and local, full of elements parishioners would see any time they looked out over the water or walked across the landscape of Isabela.

It's sunrise or sunset, with an orange sky, enhanced by clerestory windows pouring in natural light from above on either side. At the same level as the risen Christ and

to his left, the graceful fronds of six coconut palm trees extend, as if reaching toward the Christ whose arms reach toward them. The crown of each tree is heavy with green coconuts, and the trees are not idealized; some fronds are brown while others are green, suggesting that death and life are both part of this spiritual reality.

The trees grow from a green hillside with local vegetation and black volcanic rocks. A male frigate bird displays his bright-red neck balloon on one rock and a marine iguana looks out across the sea from another. The unmistakable silhouettes of flying frigate birds plus one Galápagos hawk soar together around Christ. At the horizon, where the blue Pacific Ocean meets the orange sky, a black volcano rises, silhouetted in the distance. On the right side, a sandy beach stretches to some black volcanic rocks on which are perched four Galápagos penguins, six blue-footed boobies, and another marine iguana.

Then, under the eucharistic table sits a life-sized wooden carving of a Galápagos tortoise.

Along the wall to the right of the table, stained-glass-like windows (actually, they're painted glass) convey a gentle light to the nave, but they depict no slaughtered lambs, haloed saints, or angels carrying bloody swords. Instead, there's a flamingo, a blue-footed booby, a marine iguana, a tortoise, and a penguin. On the opposite wall, two paintings also display native flora and fauna, and the third depicts the moment of creation, with a vibrant style somewhat reminiscent of William Blake's paintings, complete with the sun, planets, and moon. The message is clear: the risen Christ is with us, with us in this place, and every creation is an icon of the divine, with holy light shining through.

My companions who share the photos are not religious in the traditional sense, but I'm touched by their eagerness to share their experience of the church with me, and I sense that they are touched by the scene in ways they can't fully put into words.

I feel the same way.

JOY

Last night we motored east and north from the southern
end of Isabela, along the west coast of Santa Cruz, to
Isla Rábida, just off the southwestern coast of Santiago. I
awaken while it's still dark, and realize we've come to our
last full day.

I climb to the upper deck and see the cliffs of Rábida
rise from the sea. As the light grows stronger, I realize
that the tar-black cliffs are actually rust-red, and from the
base of the cliff stretches a long curve of red-sand beach
with vivid green saltbush bordering the red sand. Beyond

the saltbush is gray-green scrub spiked with tree cacti, and beyond the scrub, another ghost forest of palo santo trees, a bit less ghostly here because a mist of smoky green indicates they are beginning to bud. The higher up the slope, the more intense the green.

After breakfast, we take dinghies to the beach. We wander the red sand between the gentle surf and the saltbush border. Billy wanders with us, waiting for someone to notice something and ask a question, and then gathering us for an explanation. We come upon the remains of a pelican, and he tells us common ways that young pelicans die. We notice unusual tracks in the sand, and he tells us about how the sea turtles come ashore to nest. Then we disperse and roam the beach to make our own discoveries. I come upon two kinds of sea stars I haven't seen before, one red like the sand with orange spikes on the side, one wheat-colored with coffee-brown lines radiating from the center. I pick up a beautiful shell that contains a hermit crab.

Then I come to a rocky area and watch a marine iguana grazing for algae on rocks exposed by the low tide. A few bites from one side of the jaw, and then from the other, then a wave splashes over him and he moves to another spot and repeats the process. Unhurried. Unworried. There's no shortage of algae at this time of year. I picture one of his distant ancestors grazing like this, more akin to a land iguana, and I can easily envision the slow process of adaptation that would lead to this creature before me.

Our dinghy picks us up from the beach for our final snorkeling trip. We drop backward into the waves about a mile or so away, in a cove around the point, on the windward side of Rábida where the water is much rougher. We will swim along the rocky shore, around the point, and all the way back to the beach.

This snorkeling venture is by far our most challenging, a fitting way to end our time under-water. First we have big waves crashing on the rocks to our left to contend with. Then, as we round the point, we have a strong current working against us. It takes a normal amount of swimming effort just to stay in place, and real effort to progress slowly.

> I had been my whole life a bell, and never knew it until at that moment I was lifted and struck.
>
> —Annie Dillard

But we're rewarded with some of the best sea-life sightings so far.

I notice how different species are clustered in the different areas we pass through. Nearest the rocky ledge, of course, the familiar reef fish defend their little territories—damselfish, wrasses, angelfish. Large schools of cardinalfish and black-striped salema allow us to pass through them, dazzling with color and movement. A little deeper, on a mostly sandy bottom, we pass "sea-star city," an area where large five-pointed Panamic cushion stars have congregated, their bright orange-red spikes against a dark blue to black background.

In another area, several especially beautiful pyramid sea stars cling to a tower of rock. Their five slender legs

vary from mottled olive to mustard yellow. Beneath them in patches of sand I see a half-dozen rounded chocolate chip sea stars also clustered together, their bodies the color of café au lait, with a chocolate stripe running from the center to the blunt end of each broad, rounded foot, chocolate chips scattered generously between the stripes.

Near where the current runs strongest, I pass several aggregations of parrotfish of several species, bumpheads with their intense green and blue; blue-chins with their outrageous aqua, teal, hot pink, and yellow; bi-colors and azures whose myriad shades contradict their common names. How to describe them? Neon pink and neon blue? Electric aqua and psychedelic turquoise? Perhaps some things are beyond description and it's best to not even try. As I pass, I hear the crackling sound of their beaks scraping and breaking off bite-sized chunks of coral.

A larger whitetip reef shark passes through, chunky, nearly four feet long. I see my first Sierra mackerel, a sleek, silvery bullet about thirty inches long, reminiscent of a kingfish back home in the Gulf of Mexico.

The water grows shallower and the rocky bottom gives way to the red gravel and sand of the beach. My swim is almost over, I think. And just then, a young sea lion swims up and makes eye contact. He passes me and I quickly turn to keep him in view. That, it turns out, is his signal to play. He circles back and spins around me, and

I spin to keep him in view, and we continue this game in waist-deep water for several minutes. I realize he's like one of those puppies who will keep retrieving a ball as long as you keep throwing it, and I start laughing aloud through my snorkel. About then, another swimmer in our group comes up beside me. The pup zips over to her and the process begins again. As I take off my flippers and walk to the shore, I hear her laughing through her snorkel as well.

I laugh out loud once again. Joy, it turns out, is both irresistible and contagious.

We either agree with Macbeth that life is nothing more than a "tale told by an idiot," a purposeless emergence of life-forms including the clever, greedy, selfish, and unfortunately destructive species that we call *Homo sapiens*. Or we believe that, as Pierre Teilhard de Chardin put it, "There is something afoot in the universe, something that looks like gestation and birth."

—Jane Goodall *(adapted)*

While we eat lunch, we motor south to a cove on Santa Cruz. Just north of our destination, I recognize the distinctively shaped island that I saw during my original descent to Baltra, a slanted slab on the horizon. Next to it, two islands side by side, one looking like a Hershey's kiss, the other, like a half-melted Hershey's kiss.

We climb aboard the dinghies for our final hike of the voyage. We land at the base of Dragon Hill, named for the population of land iguanas that lived here long ago, then didn't, and now do again.

Before we meet one of these dragons in person, we encounter one of their cousins, a large black marine iguana, at the edge of the path, just feet from the beach. Then, not ten yards away on the inland side of the path, we hear the sound of a huge male land iguana moving through the leaves, foraging for fallen cactus fruit.

The animal itself is impressive, its head, legs, and belly a bright yellow, its back and tail saddle brown, its neck and forehead covered with enlarged, protruding scales, spiky, horn-like. On its back runs a crest of yellow-white spines maybe three-quarters of an inch long, a final touch that makes it look like a dragon or dinosaur indeed.

Equally impressive is its behavior as it crawls beneath large tree cacti. The cacti stand about twelve to fifteen feet tall and are covered in long, sharp spines, each longer than a sewing needle and almost as rigid. Their fruits are no less spiny. We watch as the iguana reaches out a foot and rubs a fallen fruit on the ground a few times, obviously trying to break off some of the longest spines. Then, with most of the spines still intact, it picks up the fruit in its mouth, chews it twice, and swallows it whole. I can only imagine the leatheriness of its tongue, mouth, and esophagus to swallow such a pincushion—not to mention the strength of its stomach acid to digest it all!

We notice several tree cacti nearby that have bent over a few feet from the ground and died. Billy points out that they all contain a hole about the size of an apple at the bend in the trunk. These holes, he explains, were made by Galápagos mockingbirds. Desperate for some fresh water in the dry season, first they pecked a small hole to extract a few drops from the cactus. They then returned to the same hole again and again until it enlarged to the point where the next storm felled the cactus.

We make our way from the arid zone into a second ecological niche, a transition zone, grassy areas mixed with a few tree cacti, palo santo trees, and other drought-tolerant trees. Here, we encounter some more land iguanas going about their daily life. One stands on his hind legs to reach a leaf. A pair lie side by side, the male in his yellow breeding splendor, the female with a buff-colored head but her body a dusty slate. From her shoulders down, she resembles a marine iguana, suggesting their common ancestry. Occasionally the male bobs his head in a half-hearted courting gesture. The female, unimpressed, moves on and chomps on some red berries she finds under a bitter melon tree.

As we stand watching them in the humid breeze, the first really warm breeze of our trip, Billy tells us the story of Dragon Island. In 1978, CDRS researchers came to survey the well-being of the animals. They were concerned because feral dogs had infested much of Santa Cruz. They found only sixty-eight land iguanas, many of them with open wounds and scars, sure signs of dog attacks. As an emergency measure, they captured and moved the iguanas to a nearby island. The iguanas thrived, but over a ten-year period, there was no successful reproduction.

The scientists realized that there was no suitable sand on this island for the females to dig burrows to bury their eggs. So they painstakingly shoveled a large amount of sand from Dragon Hill and carried it to their temporary home to create a nesting area. Their laborious plan worked, and soon, babies were growing on the island.

Unfortunately, dogs managed to swim across to the island, and soon, they were killing iguanas again. So the researchers captured all the remaining iguanas once more and transported them back to the breeding facility in Puerto Ayora.

In the coming years, the captive population of Dragon Hill iguanas continued to grow, and feral dogs were finally eliminated from Santa Cruz. Some years ago, the iguanas were repatriated to their home environment and now their numbers have grown to over four hundred.

We continue our ascent through a palo santo forest and pass burrow after burrow, dug by the iguanas for sleeping. By the time we reach the top of Dragon Hill, we have seen at least ten of the four hundred dragons.

I wish you could come here and rest a year in the simple unmingled Love fountains of God. You would then return with fresh truth gathered and absorbed from pines and waters and deep singing winds, and you would find that they all sang of fountain Love just as did Jesus Christ and all of pure God manifest in whatever form.

—John Muir *(adapted)*

As we enjoy the views and the breeze at the summit, Billy tells us another land iguana success story from Baltra, the island where most inbound air travelers land and from which we will depart the next day. Iguanas were known to live in large numbers there during a scientific survey in 1932. For some reason unknown today, those scientists took several Baltra iguanas and released them on a nearby island, North Seymour, that had no iguanas.

During World War II, Baltra, already an Ecuadorian naval base, became a major military base from which Allied forces protected the Panama Canal. Not surprisingly, soldiers found the land iguanas tasty to eat or an easy target for shooting practice. By the end of the war, the Baltra population was extinct. In 1965, scientists from the newly formed CDRS visited the Seymour population. The animals were thriving, but they had no successful reproduction. As with the Dragon Hill iguanas, they brought the survivors to CDRS and they began reproducing. About fourteen years ago, CDRS and the Ecuadorian Navy reached an agreement to protect the animals, so they were reintroduced to Baltra. Now, the population has grown to over a thousand. Some of the original animals that were removed in 1932 are still alive, demonstrating the iguana's impressive longevity.

We return to the beach, and while waiting for our dinghies, we walk along the water's edge, savoring our last few moments in the Galápagos wild. I take some video of a sea turtle swimming in the clear cove shallows. Suddenly a blue-footed booby drops behind him in a vertical dive into the sea to feed. The bird disappears for a full three seconds and then pops up like a submerged beach ball and flies away, presumably with dinner in its beak.

I have been hoping to capture that sight since the day of my arrival, and now I get it by accident at the last minute, with a sea turtle in the foreground as a bonus.

During our last dinner together, we share toasts, thanks, and lots of laughter. We each get our picture taken with the crew, which gives us a chance to give them envelopes (provided to us by Billy) that contain our tips. (Most travelers give ten to twenty dollars per traveler per day, to be divided between the guide and the crew.)

I end up at a table with three other men, the first time we have segregated by gender during the trip. We get into a deep conversation about a book read by one of our number called *Bullshit Jobs: A Theory*, by David Graeber. It leads us to talk about the meaning of work, the meaning of money, the meaning of life, and the future of humanity. Heavy conversation for our last night!

God does not appear, and flow out, only from narrow chinks and round bored wells here and there in favored races and places, but flows in grand undivided currents, shoreless and boundless over creeds and forms and all kinds of civilizations and peoples and beasts, saturating all and fountainizing all.

—John Muir *(adapted)*

I look around the galley and each table shares similarly animated conversation. Our little band has clearly bonded, become friends, discovered the differing gifts that each has to offer. We have evolved from sixteen strangers into one social ecosystem, a community of mutual respect—even affection. I realize I have unconsciously made a decision not to write about my companions in any detail, and now I understand why: I haven't wanted to stand apart from them to render them objects of my "Galápagos experience." Instead, I have chosen to share the experience with them, as fully as possible, simply one of the group.

Tomorrow, we will say goodbye, and this community will, in all likelihood, never meet again. Even if some of us return to the islands, it will be with other people, and it will be *as* other people, too, since we will all have grown and changed. This realization intensifies the preciousness of this trip, with this circle of friends, at this moment.

I get a lump in my throat as I ponder all this, and I feel afresh the joy of these final moments together in our shared adventure.

DETACHMENT

When does an adventure end? Is it when you close your bulging suitcase or board your return flight?

Or does the adventure continue as you relive memories, review photographs, and, of course, tell stories, lots of stories—in person or through writing, as I'm doing right now?

It's my last morning on the *Golondrina*, and these questions run circles in my mind as I pack my suitcase and prepare to leave the Galápagos Islands, quite possibly never to return. It's hard to believe that eight days have slipped

by. My socks from the week's excursions are still damp and stained red, black, and brown from the sands of Rábida, Santiago, and Santa Cruz. They smell so dank I wrap them in the blue plastic poncho I purchased at Rancho Manzanillo. I break a zipper on my suitcase trying to make everything fit, but fortunately there's a second zipper.

I bring my suitcase to the rear deck and notice that one of the crew members has already unmoored the dinghy.

He's drifting maybe thirty yards behind the *Golondrina*, using his phone signal to check World Cup scores. When he sees me, he starts the motor and pulls up to the ship. Soon, the dinghy is loaded with everyone's luggage, and he carries it to shore where it will be transferred to a truck that will carry it to the airport.

Then comes our turn for transport.

We put on our blue life jackets and board our dinghies for the last time. As we pull away, I take one of my favorite photos of the trip, a simple picture of the *Golondrina*, a white boat under a gray sky reflected in a smooth silver sea.

It's a short ride, maybe seven minutes.

For the last eight days we have been so focused on diving blue-footed boobies, frolicking sea lions, and cactus-eating land iguanas that we've taken relatively few photos of each other.

That changes between the *Golondrina* and the dock.

Just before we disembark, Billy jokes, "Okay. For your last piece of information in the Galápagos, I tell you this: the life jackets are not included in the cost of the trip. So please leave them in the boat." Billy climbs off first and one last time gives us the official Galápagos forearm grab to help us transfer safely from the rocking boat to the steady dock. "Safe and sound," he says. "You are on dry land. Now go home and tell all your friends to come visit us on the *Golondrina*, the best ship on the planet. No, the universe! Come see us again, amigos!"

A sign at the dock offers a similar message: *Feliz Retorno.*

I would love to visit again. But I doubt I can wait seventeen years this time. The math gets tight from sixty-two on, you know? How many years of snorkeling do I have left? How many years of hiking? How many years of breathing?

While we wait for the bus, one of my German companions and I have our best conversation of the trip. We speak of growing older. We speak of making deep connections. We speak of letting go. We embrace and say goodbye with more awareness than we had when we were younger of what goodbyes mean.

Billy rides the bus with us to the airport because he needs to meet his next group, who will be arriving on the same plane on which we will depart. "After you check in," he says, "don't go through security. It's really boring in there. There's nothing to do. Stay out here. There's a bar on the other side. Get some food. Go into the secure area at the last possible minute." We've been taking guidance from Billy for a week and it has gone well, so we don't stop now. We spend the next ninety minutes at the outdoor bar.

We pull a bunch of tables together, our last act of solidarity. We order food, chat, share photos. Some read, some write. I sit and watch the wind turbines turning for a while, pondering what they do, how they work, what they mean to the visitors who pass by. Then I notice the new arrivals fresh off the incoming flight, shifting their backpacks, consulting their guidebooks, looking for the proper bus, buzzing with a mix of nervous excitement and cluelessness.

I know what awaits them. Sea lions will frolic with them. Marine iguanas will gaze at them with the perfect Zen detachment of a stone Buddha statue. Sally Light-foot crabs will make way for them, but never much faster than necessary. I know, but these rookies can't imagine now what delights await in this mysterious place where warm and cold currents meet, where earth's tectonic plates

I think that the dying pray at the last not "please," but "thank you," as a guest thanks his host at the door. Falling from airplanes the people are crying thank you, thank you, all down the air.

—Annie Dillard

collide, where enchanted animals enchant their human sisters and brothers with natural signs and wonders, and where strangers become companions in the miracle of friendship.

A tour bus full of eager rookies revs its engine near our table and departs, baptizing my companions and me in its exhaust fumes, confirming our reentry into the so-called civilized world.

> An adventure is only an inconvenience rightly considered. An inconvenience is only an adventure wrongly considered.
>
> —G. K. Chesterton

I get out my notebook to scratch down some notes for this chapter. I can't help but notice Darwin's finches flitting around the tables, picking up crumbs, not just from tables or the patio floor, but from people's plates. Then, a wordless benediction: a Galápagos dove comes and lands on my table. He wanders among the plates and cups of my companions and settles down for a moment beside my left hand, not far from the notebook on which I'm about to describe him using my right hand.

He's small, a rich brown, his feathers slightly iridescent, with black and white feathers on his wings. He sports a truly striking turquoise ring around each eye, plus a splash of white between two black bars behind each eye, resembling the kind of punk makeup you might see at an avant-garde nightclub somewhere in the pricey section of a big modern city. I put down my pen, slowly maneuver my right hand into my pocket, find my phone, and manage to get one last photograph without scaring him away.

Well, it isn't actually my last photo. When I wander into the airport store to pick up some souvenirs for my grandkids, I see a T-shirt with one word, a fitting memento of the islands: EVOLVE.

I don't buy it, but I do photograph it. And right below it, there's another T-shirt that I also shoot:

It is not the strongest of the species that survives, nor the most intelligent that survives. It is the one that is the most adaptable to change.
—Charles Darwin

An hour later, on the plane to Guayaquil, I'm going through my photos and I pause on this quote. If Darwin is right, and I don't doubt him on this, how ironic that orthodoxies, whether religious, political, or economic, punish adaptation and fight change as evil and unfaithful. As my friend Richard Rohr says, "We often worship old things as substitutes for eternal things." What would it mean to be faithful not to the old orthodoxies of the recent past (recent in deep time, that is) but rather to the primeval patterns written forever into creation itself, the profound logic of adaptation, evolution, diversification, and symbiotic coexistence? Isn't that a deeper kind of orthodoxy?

And isn't that the ongoing graduation I'm celebrating, from the rigid orthodoxy of nostalgia and fear to the generous orthodoxy that is written like a code, a program, a *logos*, a *sophia*, into the fabric of the universe itself?

When does an adventure end?

If there are finite and infinite games, as the brilliant James Carse has written, surely there are finite and infinite

> It's a funny thing coming home. Nothing changes. Everything looks the same, feels the same, even smells the same. You realize what's changed is you.
>
> —F. Scott Fitzgerald

adventures as well. If my adventure in the Galápagos has consisted only of seeing and photographing amazing animals, plants, and landscapes, then whenever it began, I suppose it ends before I land in Guayaquil.

But even here in this modern airport, still playing Muzak and still over-air-conditioned, things look different. I notice the care taken by the designers to include a little indoor rainforest near the baggage-claim area, complete with magenta and mauve orchids, a water feature, and a wall of verdant vegetation. Outside, between the building and the busy pick-up lanes, I see a large pond in which flame-orange koi curve and brim, gill to gill in crowded schools.

We humans know that even in our cities we need connections with our original neighbors, whether they're verdant green, magenta and mauve, or flame orange. Perhaps that was the real quest of this adventure, the infinite quest for connection with everything, everyone, everywhere, always—the quest to let down my barriers, let go of my agendas and expectations, and simply be open to who and what may come, now and next.

Perhaps that is why I feel so happy now, irrationally happy at the beginning of a seven-hour layover in Guayaquil Airport: even though I have come to the end of eight profoundly wonderful days, even though my layover is long, even though I am in some ways detaching from the people I've met and the amazing creatures and landscapes I've enjoyed, I've gotten back in touch to some small degree with the infinite and eternal adventure.

And that will continue as long as I let it.

MONSTER

I've been home from my journey for a few weeks now, and I can't stop thinking about Charles Darwin. His face and story seem as endemic to the Galápagos Islands as a saddleback tortoise or flightless cormorant, even though their interconnection is a little more complicated than most folks think.

Darwin spent five weeks in the islands in late 1835, but his evolutionary eureka moments did not unfold there. Rather, his observations in the islands, along with many other observations from his long around-the-world voyage, simmered like a suspicion for literally decades. Some weeks after leaving the islands, he wrote in one of his notebooks, "If there is the slightest foundation for evolution, the zoology of the Galápagos will be well worth examining." But like the theory Darwin would articulate, that early inkling would only develop slowly and unpredictably, piece by piece, as it adapted to challenges and changes in his external environment.

In the islands, Darwin collected thirteen small birds that he assumed were wrens, finches, and grosbeaks. (*Collected* in those days meant shot and stuffed.) A few years later, after returning to London, Darwin showed them to the great ornithologist John Gould. No, Gould said when

he inspected them, they were all varieties of a ground finch. What did that mean? Similarly, what did it mean that the three different mockingbirds Darwin had collected hailed from three different islands?

Not one to rush to judgment, Darwin "kept these things and pondered them in his heart," to borrow a biblical phrase (Luke 2:19). Finally, in 1844, in a letter to Sir Joseph Hooker he dared to confide what he was coming to see: "At last gleams of light have come, and I am almost convinced (quite to the contrary to the opinion I started with) that species are not (it is like confessing a murder) immutable."[8]

He could well have committed an actual murder, based on the impression of him I gained from the conservative Christians in whose company I was raised. They saw Darwin as an arrogant, faithless, Bible-denying, God-hating, religion-murdering monster.

After all, didn't the Bible, God's inspired, inerrant word, teach the objective propositional truth that God made the earth in seven literal twenty-four-hour periods? ("Words have meanings! Day means day!" I can hear the preacher shout.) Didn't the Bible give us an accurate

---

8. Letter to Joseph Dalton Hooker from Charles Darwin, January 11, 1844, Darwin Correspondence Project, University of Cambridge, https://tinyurl.com/y4yq4356.

historical record, from Adam who begat Cain who begat Enoch who begat Irad . . . to Jesus who begat Christianity? ("If the Bible says it, I believe it, and that settles it!" the preacher boasts.) And didn't biblical arithmetic add up to a world that was not, as Darwin implied, millions or billions of years old, but rather about six thousand? ("You are descended from Adam and Eve in about 4004 BC," the preacher yells. "And you are certainly *not* descended from some pair of monkeys millions of years ago!")

Didn't the inspired, inerrant Bible teach that God destroyed all of earth's land creatures in a great flood, except for a pair of each creature preserved on Noah's ark, which means they disseminated to repopulate the world from Mount Ararat in Turkey? ("If the Bible is inspired, it's inerrant," the preacher growls, "because God doesn't inspire error!") Didn't the Bible say that God made creatures to reproduce "after their kind," without mutation, and certainly without evolution? ("All this talk of evolution— it's nothing but devil-ution!" the preacher mocks.)

Although I left behind the shallow fundamentalism of those antiscience preachers in my young-adult life, I had never actually read Darwin's *On the Origin of the Species*, apart from a few famous quotations. I decided to remedy that lapse in my education just before my voyage to the Galápagos.

My firsthand first impression of the man as I read his greatest work: Darwin seemed like one of the most dutiful, decent, earnest, sincere, detailed, logical, ethical, curious, and honest humans imaginable. (No wonder the American philosopher John Fiske described him after his death as "the dearest, sweetest, loveliest old grandpa that ever was."[9]) With painstaking care, he makes his case in *On the Origin of the Species*, baby step by baby step, page by page, drawing from a wide array of sources, from the latest research in domestic pigeon-breeding to his own observations of creatures around the world. He didn't hide from objections that seemed to challenge or undermine his theory but instead presented them fairly and faced them honestly.

As I read, it became clear that he was not simply overcoming others' objections through his painstaking research, but his own.

As a young man, Darwin was deeply influenced by clergyman William Paley, especially Paley's *Natural Theology*, which taught that the universe is designed to reveal to humanity a wise and benevolent God who works through

---

9. Thomas F. Glick, *What about Darwin?* (Baltimore: John Hopkins University Press, 2010), 119. Fiske adds, "And on the whole, he impresses me with his strength more than any man I have yet seen. There is a charming kind of quiet strength about him."

the majestic laws of nature. Paley's ideas were deeply forma-
tive for the young Darwin, and for a while, Darwin planned
to follow Paley's footsteps and become a clergyman.

But because of his passionate interest in the natural
world, from geology to beetles, when he was presented
with the opportunity to travel around the whole natural
world as an amateur naturalist on a ship named *The Beagle*
in 1835, he jumped at the opportunity, assuming he would
proceed with his theological interests after returning.

In his autobiography, Darwin wrote that during the
voyage, "I was led to think much about religion. Whilst
on board the Beagle I was quite orthodox, & I remember
being heartily laughed at by several of the officers (though
themselves orthodox) for quoting the Bible as an unanswerable authority on some point of morality."[10]

Only slowly did he begin to question the Bible as "an
unanswerable"—which means *unquestionable*—authority.
"I had gradually come, by this time, to see," he said, "that
the Old Testament from its manifestly false history of
the world, with the Tower of Babel, rainbow as a sign,
etc., etc., and from its attributing to God the feelings of
a revengeful tyrant, was no more to be trusted than the

---

10. Charles Darwin, *The Life and Letters of Charles Darwin*,
vol. 1, p. 132, Classic Literature Library, https://tinyurl.com
/y6k5lf2c.

sacred books of the Hindoos, or the beliefs of any barbarian."[11]

Early in the voyage, when he scooped up plankton in a net in the middle of the ocean, he marveled at their intricacy and beauty. But even the plankton raised theological questions for him. Why would God place them there, where no human could enjoy them? The anthropocentrism of conventional theism, inherent in William Paley's work, just didn't

> Where there is no longer any opportunity for doubt, there is no longer any opportunity for faith either.
>
> — Paul Tournier

make sense in the context of a world of such staggering size, diversity, complexity, intricacy, and fecundity.

In South America, Darwin became fascinated with fossils and participated in several important digs, but his

---

11. Charles Darwin, *The Autobiography of Charles Darwin, 1809–1882: With the Original Omissions Restored*, ed. Nora Barlow (London: Collins, 1958), 85.

fascination triggered more questions: Why would God allow so many specially created species to go extinct? If the point of creation is to display God's greatness to humanity, why display such waste through death and extinction? And if the point of humanity is its destination after death, why create so much history in which humanity played no role? Did dinosaurs in the past, like plankton in the present, matter for their own sake?

Meanwhile, although Darwin was frequently enamored with the beauty of nature, he also saw its terror, as in the fate of a caterpillar captured by a wasp to be consumed alive by the wasp's larvae. Why would a benevolent Creator design such horrific parasitism to add misery to the lives of these creatures?

Frequently in his voyage, and especially in the Galápagos Islands, Darwin saw evidence of massive geological changes, some sudden and some gradual over long stretches of time, from volcanism to earthquakes to uplifted sea floors. These observations conflicted with conventional Christian ideas of a young and stable earth, created by God in the relatively recent past. In short, the earth that Darwin was coming to understand was shockingly old and constantly changing. What did geological age and change mean for biology, anthropology, and theology?

Darwin's inherited theological beliefs—rigid, fixed, unbending—didn't fit in this universe that was growing so much larger, so much older, so much more dynamic, and so much more complex in his understanding.

His theology was, we might say, unable to adapt. It was struggling for survival because it didn't fit the world he was experiencing.

As he grappled with these scientific realities on the *Beagle*, he also grappled with new moral, social, and political complexities. In Argentina, for example, he observed firsthand the oppression and racism inherent in European Christian imperialism. Part of him was formed by the prejudices of his culture, but another part of him was appalled by the inhumanity of colonization and slavery, as illustrated in this anecdote:

Near Rio de Janeiro I lived opposite to an old lady, who kept screws to crush the fingers of her female slaves. I have stayed in a house where a young household mulatto, daily and hourly, was reviled, beaten, and persecuted enough to break the spirit of the lowest animal. . . . I will not even allude to the many heart-sickening atrocities which I authentically heard of;—nor would I have mentioned the above revolting details, had I not met with several people . . . [who] speak of slavery as a tolerable evil.[12]

The structure of his inherited Christian moral universe, in which slavery was either a God-ordained good or a tolerable evil, was crumbling right along with his inherited prescientific Christian worldview.

After his voyage, he fell in love with his first cousin Emma and proposed marriage (not an uncommon arrangement in those days). He confided his religious doubts to his fiancée, and she was concerned, though grateful for his honesty. She wrote in a personal letter:

My reason tells me that honest & conscientious doubts cannot be a sin, but I feel it would be a painful void between us. I thank you from my heart for your openness with me & I should dread the feeling that you were concealing your opinions from the fear of giving me pain. It is perhaps

---

12. Charles Darwin, *Journal of Researches into the Natural History and Geology of the Countries Visited during the Voyage of H.M.S. Beagle Round the World* (New York: D. Appleton, 1871), 499–500, https://tinyurl.com/y62x4nm8. It's also worth noting that Darwin learned how to stuff birds from a former slave, about whom he wrote: "I used often to sit with him, for he was a very pleasant and intelligent man." Darwin, *Autobiography*, 51.

foolish of me to say this much but my own dear Charley we now do belong to each other & I cannot help being open with you. Will you do me a favour? yes I am sure you will, it is to read our Saviours farewell discourse to his disciples which begins at the end of the 13th Chap of John. It is so full of love to them & devotion & every beautiful feeling. It is the part of the New Testament I love best. This is a whim of mine it would give me great pleasure, though I can hardly tell why I don't wish you to give me your opinion about it.[13]

Here, I must acknowledge, Emma demonstrated exactly the three-step process I myself have employed in my own faith evolution. First, she acknowledged that honest doubt can't be a sin. Then, she centered her faith on Jesus and simultaneously de-centered passages from the Bible that make dubious claims—whether a young earth created in seven days or the divine command to commit genocide against the Canaanites. And finally, she gave her primary focus to Jesus's teachings of love, as evidenced, for example, in John's Gospel.

---

13. Letter to Charles Darwin from Emma Wedgwood, November 1838, Darwin Correspondence Project, University of Cambridge, https://tinyurl.com/y4lrj2j5.

> The time of the Scopes monkey trial was also the height of lynching. Why were White American Christians so up in arms about evolution but so silent about lynching?
>
> —Xavier Pickett *(paraphrased)*

Yet Emma suspected that even this approach to faith that worked for her might not prove satisfying to her beloved Charley with his "honest and conscientious" mind.

In the end, Emma's suspicion proved accurate.

For a while after their wedding in 1839, the Darwin family attended Anglican services (although Emma was herself Unitarian). But by 1849, after walking with Emma and their children to the gate of the church, Darwin would turn and take a quiet stroll alone while they participated in the liturgy inside. In 1851, when their beloved daughter Annie died, Darwin's faith was pushed further over the edge. He felt no consolation in the idea of heaven, and the idea of hell repulsed him. He later wrote in his posthumously published autobiography,

I can indeed hardly see how anyone ought to wish Christianity to be true; for if so the plain language of the text seems to show that the men who do not believe, and this would include my Father, Brother and almost all my best friends, will be everlastingly punished. And this is a damnable doctrine.[14]

Emma and their son Francis, aware that pious people would use passages like this one to vilify Charles and discredit his life's work, removed all such critical statements about religion when the autobiography was originally published in 1887.

In fact, it wasn't until 1958, seventy-six years after Charles's death, that Emma and Charles's granddaughter, Nora Barlow, included the excised passages in a new edition.

Emma and Francis were justified in their fears: the pious did indeed portray Charles as a faith-killing, theocidal monster, as they still do today. I heard many anti-Darwin sermons in my youth, a century after his death, and my well-meaning parents made sure that for many a birthday, their science-obsessed teenage son received books published by the Institute for Creation Research, from whom you can still buy books with titles like these:

Twenty Evolutionary Blunders: Dangers and Difficulties of Darwinian Thinking

---

14. Darwin, *Autobiography*, 87.

The Long War against God
Five Minutes with a Darwinist: Exposing the
   FLUFF of Evolution
How Darwinism Corrodes Morality
C. S. Lewis: Anti-Darwinist
Hitler and the Nazi Darwinian Worldview[15]

Darwin himself would probably be best described in his later years as an agnostic, not an atheist. (By the way, a story widely circulated in the 1950s about Darwin's deathbed evangelical conversion—I heard it in sermons as a boy—was rejected by Darwin's family as a completely unfounded tale, "fabricated in the USA."[16])

In 1873, less than a decade before his death, he wrote in a personal letter:

I may say that the impossibility of conceiving that this grand and wondrous universe, with our conscious selves, arose through chance, seems to

---

15. See "Search results for Darwin," Institute of Creation Research, accessed July 5, 2018, https://tinyurl.com/y4r8ljmc. Another article on a similar site ends, "Darwin did indeed have a cause . . . the abolition of God." Russell Grigg, "Darwin, Slavery, and Abolition," Creation.com, April 2011, https://tinyurl.com/yxf3d2pn.
16. Wikipedia, s.v. "Deathbed Conversion," https://tinyurl.com/pvddem8.

me the chief argument for the existence of God; but whether this is an argument of real value, I have never been able to decide. I am aware that if we admit a first cause, the mind still craves to know whence it came from and how it arose. Nor can I overlook the difficulty from the immense amount of suffering through the world. I am, also, induced to defer to a certain extent to the judgment of many able men who have fully believed in God; but here again I see how poor an argument this is. The safest conclusion seems to me to be that the whole subject is beyond the scope of man's intellect; but man can do his duty.[17]

Each leaning toward belief is interrupted by a *but*, with the final *but* leading to a call to duty.

And that perfectly matches the dominant impression I had of Darwin after reading *On the Origin of the Species*: Darwin was a dutiful man. He felt the duty of loyalty to his family, his nation, his culture, his tradition—and to the actual observable data presented to him by the world itself, including his memorable trip to the Galápagos Islands.

---

17. Letter to N. D. Doedes from Charles Darwin, April 2, 1873, Darwin Correspondence Project, University of Cambridge, https://tinyurl.com/y6mztz5f.

And where these competing loyalties were in tension, he was loyal to the tension itself. He lived with it, felt it, and refused to resolve it.

When I read portions of Darwin's autobiography, and even more in biographical portraits written by others, I was struck by how that unresolved tension must have contributed to Darwin's terrible health in his later years. Stomach problems (he once vomited for twenty-seven straight days) often rendered him an invalid and Emma his nurse.[18] He faced the horrible reality that if he spoke the truth as he had come to see it, he would be misunderstood and hated; and even more agonizing, his ideas could be abused by unscrupulous people to justify injustices

> In the past Christianity meant a flight from the world. In an evolutionary universe, however, it is a flight from separateness.
>
> —Ilia Delio

---

18. "On the Origin of Species," *Encyclopaedia Britannica Online*, s.v. "Charles Darwin," https://tinyurl.com/y8w8rx5r.

that he morally abhorred, like slavery or economic exploitation of the poor by the rich.

That dutiful and agonizing fidelity may not be a Sunday-school definition of faith, but it strikes me as a pretty dependable definition of faithfulness, and it portrays dutiful and agonized Charley Darwin not as a monster but as a good and decent man of conscience, struggling to do the right thing at the right time in the right way.

If there are monstrous and indecent characters in the story, they would be those who have carelessly and dishonestly vilified this good man for a century and a half in the name of piety and tradition.

Anyone who investigates Darwin's story fairly and honestly will agree: he was no iconoclastic rebel, brash, bold, and eager to challenge every convention. No, he worked patiently and painstakingly for twenty years to test his argument and face every objection, from the theory's inception by 1839, to his first intention to write on the subject in 1844, to his firm decision to begin what he considered a short book on the subject in 1854, to the final publication of *On the Origin of the Species* in 1859.

In his masterful book *The Song of the Dodo*, David Quammen tells the story of another naturalist and world traveler, Alfred Russel Wallace. A younger contemporary of Darwin's, Wallace independently reached conclusions nearly identical to his in 1855. In fact, Wallace's plans to publish his freshly brewed ideas pushed Darwin to finally put his own slow-cooked theory in print. Darwin's dutiful, painstaking care in perfecting *On the Origin of the Species* nearly meant that the title of "father of evolutionary theory" went to Wallace rather than to him.

As I reflect on Darwin's life, I drift back to a speaking engagement several years ago at St. Gregory of Nyssa Episcopal Church in San Francisco. The church is deservedly well-known for many reasons, among them a beautiful practice of dancing around the eucharistic table in the circular rotunda. While worshipers dance, another circle of dancers is pictured above them in a striking mural by artist Mark Dukes. A twelve-foot Christ leads the dance, and joining him are suns, moons, stars, four animals, and ninety larger-than-life-sized saints.[19]

Among the dancing saints is Charles Darwin, his head bald, his beard long and white, his eyebrows shaggy, and his eyes sad or serious or both.

Jesus himself, I would venture to say, would be proud to have Darwin pictured as one of his dancing companions. After all, their life's work was similar, as if they were moving to the same rhythm. They both challenged the

---

19. You can learn more and watch a video of the mural at "Dancing Saints," St. Gregory of Nyssa Episcopal Church, https://tinyurl.com/y4bm3lfl.

> Religious experience is dynamic, fluid, effervescent, yeasty. Then, when the experience quiets down, the mind draws a bead on it and extracts concepts, notions, dogmas, so that religious experience can make sense to the mind.
>
> —Howard Thurman *(adapted)*

long-established and nearly universally affirmed understandings of God. They both dared to utter, after a pious truism, the revolutionary word *but*. They both dared to say aloud the simple but revolutionary truth that what is has not always been, and what is will not always be.

And they both were seen by some as monsters for doing so.

Of course, I thought of Darwin often during my Galápagos voyage, but most poignantly one cloudy morning in Puerto Ayora when I arose early and sat on the ship's upper deck. A Darwin's finch, soot-black in body and of a specific beak-shape and variety that I couldn't distinguish, came and landed beside me, looking for crumbs. I took two photographs of him, just four feet from where I sat.

In the first photograph, he is perched at the top of a short ladder, useful to human passengers who wish to descend from the unshaded part of the upper deck to a covered area three steps down, where there was a small table and bench that served as my impromptu writing nook for the voyage.

In the second photograph, the finch is hopping down to the first step of the ladder.

His wings are down, his feet extended for a landing, and he is a black blur of motion. The blur, I suppose, could be seen as a fault in the photograph or a failure of the photographer.

Now I can't help but see the blur as the point.

ICHTHEOLOGY

Some years ago, I heard of a secret, invitation-only society. I wished and hoped that I might receive an invitation to join.

The group was started decades earlier by a Lutheran theologian and seminary professor, Pat Keifert. Pat is one of the smartest humans I've met, and I've met a lot. Many people come to me with their vexing questions about life, meaning, history, spirituality, and God. Pat is someone I go to with my own vexing questions.

At some point along the way, Wes Granberg-Michaelson joined Pat as a coleader of the group, and I put Wes in the same category as Pat, truly extraordinary as a human being, as a leader, as a thinker. Wes has led an important American denomination (the Reformed Church in America), written several significant books, and been a global ecumenical networker, linking faith leaders across traditions around issues of justice, peace, and the common good. He is also a wonderful friend.

Pat, Wes, and others in this secret society were brought together by twin passions: theology and fly-fishing.

And because I shared those passions (although back then, I was a very inexperienced fly-fisherman), I hoped an invitation might come.

Now I should say that an added bonus to the invitation is the location of the group's annual midsummer gatherings: Yellowstone National Park. I had been there briefly on a family cross-country vacation when my kids were small, but not since. Even after that short visit, I felt that the place was (to use a word associated with the Galápagos Islands) enchanted, and I hoped I could someday return.

In Yellowstone, it's not tortoises, sea lions, marine iguanas, or equatorial penguins you hope to see, but grizzly bears, elk, wolves, and bison. Their intrigue is intensified not by their Edenic friendliness, as in the Galápagos

Islands, but by the fact that many of them will kill you, and some will eat you, if you give them the chance.

I finally received the hoped-for invitation, and within hours of my arrival in Yellowstone, I was (I'm so sorry) thoroughly hooked.

The primary attraction for anglers in Yellowstone is cutthroat trout. They are beautiful to behold indeed. Their base color ranges from olive to copper to hay-bale gold to sunset orange, and they sport dark maroon to brown to black spots that usually grow more numerous toward the tail. They often have a blood-orange mark on the gill plate, but they get their name from two bright orange to blood-orange gash-marks just under their chin. To see a cutthroat glistening in dancing patterns of water-refracted light—well, it's one of the best things.

The romance of cutthroat trout is further enhanced by the neighborhoods in which they live, like the pristine streams of Yellowstone, running cold with ice-melt, tumbling among boulders through lush green valleys beneath rugged cliffs and between craggy mountains.

I forgot to mention: the name of this secret society of fly-fishing theologians is (prepare to groan) *Ichtheology*.

That's not a misspelling of ichthyology, the study of fish, but a play on words, fusing the study of fish with the study of God. Each morning, we gather and talk theology. Then in the afternoon and through the long dusk of

midsummer, we embark on our ichthyological pursuits in Soda Butte Creek, the Lamar River, and elsewhere in and near the park.

My first week in Yellowstone with these skilled and congenial fisherfolk thoroughly indoctrinated me in this fundamental conviction: the two, fish and God, go together like fish and water.

There's something about capturing a fish that feels both primal and holy, especially when I'm not fishing to get dinner, but "for sport" or for "catch and release," as it's called. When a fish takes my artificial fly, whether it's a trout in Yellowstone or a tarpon in the Everglades, I feel that the line could be an electric cord, transferring the animal's aliveness, its vital energy, its élan, like a current through my arm to my body and my soul.

The truth is that I don't actually fish just "for sport," as if fishing were a competition that involved me winning over the fish (or over other fishermen, although sometimes, that element is certainly present). Nor do I fish simply to catch and release. No, I fish for this sense of connection—to know the fish by feeling its power, its resistance, its strength, its aliveness.

I imagine that photographers feel something similar when they "catch" a moment, and so do sculptors and songwriters and poets and filmmakers. We "take" a photo. We "capture" something in sculpture or words or music or film. Even cooks, I imagine, feel they're connecting with the power of spices and vegetables and fruits and other elements of their recipes—knowing the ingredients, *catching* their inner power, and then *releasing* it for others to savor.

Whether we consume that power by literally eating it or we take it in figuratively, we are making a connection, and in that connection there is a kind of holy communion, infusion, impartation, even transubstantiation, if you will.

The old Scottish novelist (and Canadian Governor General) John Buchan famously said, "The charm of fishing is that it is the pursuit of what is elusive but attainable, a perpetual series of occasions for hope."[20] For some people, God seems easily attainable, as familiar as a lucky coin in the pocket, as conjurable as steam from a teapot. But for many of us, God is more elusive, and at best, we hope God is there, here, in here, but we can claim no rational certainty. In this way, encountering God is a lot like encountering a cutthroat trout that you can't see. You can place yourself in a suitable location, prepare yourself, reach out your line, and—wait. And hope. And wait. And hope some more. And wait some more.

Through this hopeful waiting and occasional encounter, fisherfolk get to know fish, especially fly anglers who pursue trout. They get to know where trout lie in a stream, behind or beside which boulders, beneath which riffles, and along which seams in the flow. They get to know when trout like to feed and rest, in relation to the sun, the moon, the wind, the season, and the weather. They get to know how trout hunt, whether by waiting in ambush for

20. John Buchan, *Great Hours in Sport* (London: Thomas Nelson, 1928), 15.

Knowing means more than a way to tame reality. To know is to enter into communion with things. That is why St. Augustine said, following in Plato's wake, "We know in proportion as we love."
— Leonardo Boff

the conveyor-belt current to bring them food, or by cruising from place to place. Anglers certainly get to know what trout are feeding on, often by snatching a passing insect in flight and identifying it as a mayfly, stonefly, caddis fly, or midge, or by turning over stones in a stream and identifying the insect nymphs that hide there.

And even with all this knowledge, sometimes they're skunked. ("That's why they call it fishing and not catching," someone on the shore says, feeling clever and original, while experienced fishermen roll their eyes.)

The frequency of failure has two important effects: it keeps us humble and it keeps trout mysterious.

The whole mysterious, humbling experience of fly-fishing certainly has a religious feel to it. There are the vestments of waders, vests, boots, and hats. There are the sacred objects of rods and reels, line and flies, and, of course, the elusive, unseen fish themselves. There are the ritual motions of false casting to load the rod, the power cast, the drop, the drift, the mend, the lift, the double-haul. There is the telling of sacred stories about the big one, the one that got away, that special day when everything went right, that other day when everything went hilariously wrong.

You think about this long enough and you aren't surprised that Jesus chose fishermen as his first disciples, or that among the earliest Christian symbols was the fish.

There was one fish encounter I had in the Galápagos Islands that keeps coming back to me. Each day during our snorkeling outings, we encountered amazing fish by the thousands. To see one cardinalfish glowing like a coal ember is wonder enough, but to swim in a school of shimmering orange embers is downright magical. To see a single Cortez rainbow wrasse is a gift, but to see harem after harem on outcropping after outcropping, each with a terminal male among them, is like becoming a billionaire after being a pauper all your life. You can hardly take it in.

I suppose that's what made this one encounter so special, so unique.

The first few days of our trip, after each dive, several of us pored over a book on reef fishes from the *Golondrina*'s bookshelf: "Okay, I saw that one," "And I saw that one," "I saw several of those." By the third or fourth day, we had identified so many species that we started leafing through the book before our dives to take note of species we hadn't yet seen.

And one fish in the book captivated me: the guinea-fowl puffer. As its name suggests, this species has the ability to inflate with water (or, if removed from the water, with air). When it isn't inflated (which is most of the time), it looks a bit like a big black lemon, roughly the size of a football: an oval with protruding white teeth on one end and a paintbrush-shaped tail on the other.

The guinea-fowl coloration, though, is what attracted me. The base color of the fish resembles the darkest chocolate, and it is flecked with tiny white or beige spots, resembling its namesake bird. I made a mental note of its name and decided to keep my eyes open for it.

It was on day seven that I finally saw it, during our last snorkeling excursion, beneath the red cliffs of Isla Rábida. I was snorkeling alone in an area with huge slabs of volcanic rock that had fallen into the water, creating all kinds of nooks and crannies for fish to hide.

And there she was. I saw her for less than two seconds. She was maybe eight feet below me, suspended outside a little cave, silky, delicate, precious, hovering in a shaft of sunlight. Then she vanished.

I would estimate I spent a total of twelve to fifteen hours in the water observing sea life during the trip, mask on, breathing through a snorkel. So that momentary encounter made up something like 0.003 percent of my time underwater. Yet the insistent image of her suspended outside her cave for that instant hasn't faded at all. Even now, when I close my eyes and conjure her in my imagination, she is not just an image, but an icon, a bit like Charles Darwin dancing with Jesus on the rotunda of St. Gregory of Nyssa Episcopal Church.

She hovers in my mind as an ichtheological icon of God.

One of my favorite philosopher/theologians, John Caputo, says that whether or not God exists, God *insists*. In other words, the existence of this or that God may be doubted and debated, but the *insistence of God*, the refusal of the idea of God to just fade away like alchemy or phlogiston or cassette tapes, can hardly be doubted.

When I was younger, it was pure joy to talk about God. But as I get older, I confess that talking about God is getting increasingly uncomfortable, even painful at times.

That's an embarrassing thing to admit for a guy who has made his living writing and speaking words, often about God. But there it is. I said it.

All this has been made worse by the particularly noxious way that religious leaders, especially in my troubled religion and in my troubled nation, have been using God-talk to justify the morally unjustifiable and elect the morally fetid. (In so doing, they are being faithful to a gruesome American tradition that stretches back to the slaughter of the Native peoples and the institution of slavery, both "justified" by long lists of Bible verses and pious preacherly rationalizations.)

Perhaps at some time in the future, it will become simple to speak again of God without feeling the need to gargle with mental mouthwash afterward.[21] But right now it's hard, for me at least. It feels like plastering a series of grossly enlarged, badly tinted photographs of the guineafowl puffer on a thousand big billboards along the cliffs

---

21. In my first book (*The Church on the Other Side* [Grand Rapids: Zondervan, 2000], 88), I quoted Dietrich Bonhoeffer, who said that the German church of his day had "been fighting . . . only for its self-preservation" and had thus rendered its theological vocabulary nearly meaningless. Because of the church's large-scale complicity in the face of Nazism, Bonhoeffer felt that for some period of time, "the Christian cause will be a silent and hidden affair," limited to "prayer and righteous action." Dietrich Bonhoeffer, *Letters and Papers from Prison* (New York: Macmillan, 1971), 299–300. I then quoted Southern novelist Walker Percy (*Church on the Other Side*, 92), who said something similar about the American church's complicity in the face of racism: religious leaders have so debased and trivialized their message that they "might as well be shouting Exxon! Exxon! for all anyone pays attention." Walker Percy, *The Message in the Bottle* (New York: Farrar, Straus & Giroux, 1954), 118. All these years later, I feel this ambivalence about God-talk even more acutely.

> The vision comes and goes, mostly goes, but I live for it, for the moment when the mountains open and a new light roars in spate through the crack, and the mountains slam.
>
> —Annie Dillard

of Rábida. What's the point? Each billboard cheapens the subject and debases it to the level of a tourist trap selling crappy souvenirs and dud fireworks.

The truth is that my daily "background experience" of God, as I understand God, runs deep and strong, as natural to me after all these years as my pulse, breath, sight, hearing. Yet I must admit that more intense experiences of God, validating experiences that in some way have surprised or shaken me, have been brief. Elusive. Probably filling far less than 0.003 percent of my total lived experience.

Yet God insists.

The German poet Rainer Maria Rilke touched this insistence by picturing God as a "primordial tower" around which his life revolved unceasingly, "in widening circles that reach out across the world." His endless circling endowed him not with answers about God but with insistent questions about himself: "am I a falcon, a storm, or a great song?"[22] And that is how God has insisted in my life: a centering singularity whose gravity holds me in insistent orbit, pulling me deeper into mystery, pondering who I am and what my life means.

That something so precious, so mysterious, so utterly fine as a guineafowl puffer could at this moment be moving gently to the rhythm of the waves among the submerged rock slabs of Rábida—it affects me here, in this clean, well-lit, air-conditioned place thousands of miles away. It insists to me that beauty, mystery, and fineness exist in the world, even if hidden from my view at the moment by the pollution of sleazy politicians and the latest religious scandal or sell-out in the news.

The guineafowl puffer has become part of my background experience of the world.

---

22. Rainer Maria Rilke, *Rilke's Book of Hours: Love Poems to God*, trans. Anita Barrows and Joanna Macy (New York: Riverhead, 1996), 48.

EVOTHEOLOGY

When I boarded my flight for the Galápagos Islands, along with my suitcase and computer bag, I carried an invisible suitcase into which was stuffed a heavy load of mixed and unresolved feelings. Most of those feelings were associated with religion.

I have been a God-guy virtually all my life. You might say that was inevitable, being raised in the context of conservative white American Christianity as I was. I was singing Bible songs and memorizing Bible verses before I could read. My skinny boyhood butt sat in a well-padded church pew two or three times a week. On Friday nights I went to Bible club, and in the summers I went to Bible camp. My dad led the family in Bible reading and family devotions almost every night at dinner. One way or another, a religious upbringing like that makes an impression.

Not only that, but a religious upbringing like that causes special problems for a young boy who is interested in science and history. My religion placed me in a universe where ultimate reality consisted of eternally unchanging substances or essences: God, heaven, hell, spirits, souls. Meanwhile, everything in my embodied earthly experience was about constantly changing processes, beginning with those tadpoles developing on my kitchen table when I was a boy.

My daily life was an unfolding story, an unpredictable drama about growing, making mistakes, learning lessons, getting sick, getting better, gaining, losing, and growing some more. But on Sundays, we would sing about a changeless eternal state of perfection called heaven, in which Nothing. Would. Ever. Happen. Again. Forever and ever, amen. Passing from this fascinating life to an everlasting church service was better than hell, I supposed, but still.

By the time I started learning in school about the big bang and the expanding universe, the formation of the earth and plate tectonics, biological evolution and human history, my instincts told me that I was not a good fit for this sort of religion long-term. "I'm fourteen," I remember thinking. "Four more years and I'm out of here."

If it weren't for a series of intense spiritual experiences that came shortly thereafter, I probably would have left the whole shebang. What kept me on the religious path was not the fundamentalist God presented to me boxed and shrink-wrapped in sermons, books, and songs. It was the holy and utterly loving presence I felt one night under a starry sky. It was the connection and flow I felt in deep human encounter. It was the creative spirit I felt when I composed music or poetry or opened myself to authentic art. It was the aliveness I felt running like a current through me and the world. And it was the revolutionary kindness, compassion, boldness, justice, and brilliance that danced in the stories of Jesus, beckoning me into the dance.

From my teenage years on, I read the Bible through the lens of this experience rather than the opposite—or perhaps better said, I read the Bible and my experience in light of one another. That simple unconscious habit doomed me to be forever on the fringes if not the exterior of conservative religious life, in which a literalistic reading of the Bible reigns supreme and trumps all contrary experience.

For that reason, even though I loved God, even though I left my first career as a college English teacher to become a church planter and pastor, even though after leaving

> Nature is ever at work building and pulling down, creating and destroying, keeping everything whirling and flowing, allowing no rest but in rhythmical motion, chasing everything in endless song out of one beautiful form into another.
>
> —John Muir

the pastorate I have devoted myself to the well-being of churches, my feelings toward religion have always twisted and turned with considerable ambivalence because of my conservative upbringing. To me, God means holy, loving presence, connection and flow, deep encounter and creativity, and the very human aliveness dancing in Christ, but religion means something so different I often find the two irreconcilable.

I could best sum up my experience of conservative religion in one word.

Pressure.

Pressure to avoid being punished or punishable—if not by adults, by the Supreme Adult. Pressure to be morally perfect and doctrinally right in the eyes of God and the religious authority figures who represent him (a fitting pronoun in that context). Pressure to be different and set apart from "sinners" and "the world," and especially "the liberals." Pressure to evangelize and convert everyone I can so they will go to heaven with us. Pressure to be vigilant against science and "secular" education because they dare to challenge our inerrant Bible. Pressure to be grateful for the amazing grace that saved a wretch like me (and would damn everybody else). Pressure to keep my inner being under strict vigilance and control because I could at any moment slip into desire, which could mean slipping into sin. Pressure not to question because questioning could lead to doubt and doubt could lead to heresy and heresy could lead to hell. Literally.

Conservative white American Christianity bequeathed me with such a legacy of pressure that I understood why many of my friends had thrown the whole Christian package in the dumpster and then set the whole thing on fire in a conflagration of atheism or agnosticism. Although I wanted to pass God and love and Jesus and joy and humility and wonder on to my children and grandchildren, I certainly did not want to pass on conservative white American Christianity.

I couldn't buy it all, but I couldn't throw it all away either.

My predicament evoked a brief parable from the lips of Jesus (Matthew 13:44), which I could tweak slightly to make my own: "The kingdom of heaven is like treasure hidden in a suitcase, which someone found and hid; then in his joy he goes and sells all that he has and buys that suitcase and carries it around for the rest of his life."

Yes, even in my sixties I still cherish the treasure. But every year, the suitcase becomes heavier and heavier with the dirty laundry of Christianity's past, to which it keeps adding new embarrassments and outrages constantly. Meanwhile, ice caps are melting, authoritarian klepto-crats around the world are making a killing, neo-Nazis and white supremacists are marching, and I smell smoke everywhere. To put it in Charles Darwin's terms, my inherited religion does not seem well adapted to its dete-riorating environment. And worse, in too many ways it seems to be accelerating the deterioration.

So for eight days in the Galápagos Islands, I swam in everything I loved about God. It was genuinely ecstatic.

But what to do with the suitcase?

I didn't resolve that question on my voyage. In fact, the question has only intensified in the weeks since I returned, especially when I quiet myself and descend into contemplation.

There, I hear the gentle voice of my inner guineafowl puffer, a voice that normally hides within the rocks and caves of my deepest unconscious and only occasionally ventures out into the sparkling subaquatic light of day. It echoes Charles Darwin and counters my suitcase question with a different question entirely: "What is your duty now? What is yours to do next?"

"I don't know," I answer. "That's what has me so confused. If I speak about God, especially as a privileged white Christian male, I feel like I'm adding cheap words that are instantly swallowed up in the raucous white noise of angry talk radio, repetitive cable news, predictable religious broadcasting, and manipulative religious-right politicking. But if I'm silent, I feel . . . irresponsible. Defeated. Complicit. I'm stuck neck-deep in an ethical dilemma."

> There is something in every one of you that waits and listens for the sound of the genuine in yourself. It is the only true guide you will ever have.
>
> — Howard Thurman

The voice from the caves keeps listening, inviting me to keep speaking, even though I don't know what else to say, until this comes: "There's also this: even if I speak, I'm not sure anyone is listening. And if I'm silent, I'm pretty sure plenty of other people will say what I would have said. And they'll probably say it better. Even if I do speak and a few people listen, we're still outnumbered by millions of others—actually, billions of others—who will think we're nuts. And they have huge amounts of money and huge arsenals of weapons to back up their agenda."

"So you've lost hope," the puffer whispers provocatively, "and you're giving up."

"No, no!" I shout back, holding in my tears. "Whether or not I have hope, I can't give up. I can't stand idly by and let the rich and powerful grow more so at the expense of the poor and vulnerable. I can't let them slaughter the tortoises and toxify the oceans and destroy the coral reefs and drive to extinction the cardinalfish and Cortez rainbow wrasses and—you. I love you. I do. My hope may be faltering, and my faith may be feeble, but my love is stronger than ever." As I pause to catch my breath, the tears I've been restraining overflow.

Now I wait and listen, listen and wait, to see if anything will arise from the depths.

Then the voice from the underwater cave speaks again. At first, I'm not sure if she's talking to me or to herself or to the universe.

Humans are so upset about religion and what a mess it has become. But what else could it be, composed as it is of humans struggling along in their evolutionary path? What part of human life isn't caught up in this struggle of growth and adaptation? Is politics pure, or economics? Is science pristine? Are music, education, sport, or entertainment untainted by their own types of corruption and tawdriness? Is family life free of dysfunction and harm? Isn't everything human, everything alive, torn between growth and decay, entropy and evolution?

Why are you so disillusioned? What were you expecting? Might the problem be less about the realities of religion that are causing you such disillusionment, and more about your expectations of religion that are so unrealistic? What would happen if you dropped those unrealistic expectations of religion and started expecting it to act exactly as it is acting—fearful, reactive, self-protecting, and thoroughly beholden to its major donors? What would happen then?

This barrage of personal questions catches me by surprise.

Her questions evoke an almost-forgotten memory, a memory of reading about Galápagos tortoises when I was a boy. Back then, the dominant theory proposed that regular-sized tortoises floated to the islands long ago, and once they landed, the largest in each new generation were selected by evolutionary processes, eventually producing today's giants that weigh 250 to 500 pounds. But that theory fell from favor as giant tortoise fossils kept turning up around the world. For example, in Florida where I live, fossils of tortoises equal in size to today's Galápagos species have been unearthed. In Queensland, Australia, more fossils of a similar size were found from an extinct tortoise equipped with a full set of horns protruding from its head. Even more impressive were gargantuan fossils found across southern Asia: four-thousand-pound, seven-foot-long, shelled monsters.

The new theory proposes that giant tortoises thrived for millions of years in suitable climates around the world, but as soon as humans arrived and exploited them as an easy food source, they were driven to extinction. Giant tortoises persisted in only two places, the Galápagos Islands in the Pacific Ocean and the Aldabra Atoll in the Indian Ocean, simply because voracious humans didn't arrive until more recently. When our species did arrive, the extinction process devolved as quickly there as it had elsewhere.

But this time, other humans intervened and protected the tortoises. Why? Because lately, a sufficient number of humans have evolved, not biologically, but culturally, perhaps even spiritually. Their behavior is increasingly guided

by a sense of moral responsibility to conserve, protect, cherish, and save, rather than by a singular drive to take, exploit, kill, and destroy.

Could religion itself, I wonder, be like a giant tortoise, about to go extinct at the hands of some humans, while others try to save it?

Or could religion itself be evolving, splitting into two distinct species, one a chaplaincy to an extractive economy that justifies taking, exploiting, killing, and destroying, and the other a new mutation whose primary aim is to conserve, protect, cherish, and save? Could it be increasingly fruitless to think of religion in general, or any single religion, as a single thing, because religion and religions are undergoing a process of evolutionary speciation, like tortoises, iguanas, or finches on the Galápagos Islands? And if religion is evolving, as it most certainly is, wouldn't our concepts of God also be evolving?

Deep within me, my inner guineafowl puffer hovers, and with each movement of her gills, she breathes out another question in response to the questions I'm already asking.

Can't you see how every God-concept—including yours—functions as a feature of cultural evolution, part of a survival strategy to help populations survive and maybe even thrive for a decade or century or two in challenging, changing environments?

Isn't worshiping a God-concept a way of celebrating the values shared by the community, concentrating those values into a personified whole? Isn't worship a way of projecting an idealized image for the population to emulate and imitate and please? And in that way, whether or not an actual God created the universe, isn't it inevitable that the human element in the universe would create any number of God-concepts as an evolutionary survival strategy?

Pierre Teilhard de Chardin (1881–1955) wrote: "Everything that rises must converge." In other words, evolution moves toward unity. Along the way there will be differentiation and complexity, but paradoxically, that increased complexity moves life to a greater level of unity at a higher level, until in the end there is only God who is "all in all" (see 1 Corinthians 15:28).

— Richard Rohr

Wouldn't worried capitalists inevitably project a Prosperity Gospel Candy-Man God, pouring out magical lucky breaks and insider-trading information on anxious producers and consumers? Wouldn't the downtrodden and resentful inevitably project a Violent and Vengeful Retaliator God, inspiring and empowering terrorists to fulfill their revenge fantasies? Wouldn't the privileged and powerful inevitably project an Authoritarian Law-and-Order Patriarch, perfectly designed to intimidate the potentially rebellious into fearful compliance? Wouldn't white colonizers, racists, and enslavers inevitably project a White Supreme Being to justify their schemes for supremacy? And wouldn't the hopelessly disempowered inevitably project a Postmortem Compensation Deity to bathe them in the necessities and luxuries selfishly hoarded in this life by the rich and powerful?

I'm nodding in agreement, but then I feel her turn her gaze on me.

And wouldn't the ecologically anxious project a Green Gardening God who has a personal interest in every endangered species and threatened ecosystem? And wouldn't those suffering under various forms of hate and injustice, along with their allies, inevitably project a Loving Liberator God who actively mobilizes people for nonviolent resistance against exploitation and scapegoating? And wouldn't the contemplative and introverted inevitably project a Generative Divine Presence who meets them in solitude and silence? Why are you so afraid of admitting that projection isn't something to be embarrassed about but simply an evolutionary survival strategy to be expected?

She's right. These evolutionary adaptations are as much to be expected as the elephant's lengthening trunk or the finch's adapting beak. And she's also right: I am indeed afraid of admitting that all God-concepts are, in part at least, human projections. And she's no less right to imply that her proposals apply as much to me as to the self-seeking televangelists and religious-right sycophants who so frequently embarrass and disgust me.

Ouch. Perhaps that's what I'm afraid of. Of being no different from them. Which means losing any sense of moral superiority. Which is one of the things I find most repulsive in people like them. Wow. My inner guineafowl puffer knows how to hurt a guy.

Predictably, part of me objects and wants to argue: "Hold it. Just because something is useful for survival doesn't make it true. Shouldn't I care about what's true? Shouldn't I care if my preferred God-concept is in or out of sync with ultimate reality?" I'm a little embarrassed by the desperate tone of my voice, but then again, I'm speaking from my desperate heart.

The gentle voice from the depths responds, but seems oblivious to my questions.

It's not just explicitly religious humans who engage in this personification of desired or needed attributes. Even secular and atheist humans do the same thing. Think of the economists' Invisible Hand of the Market and the moral wonders it performs, rewarding the industrious, punishing the lazy and under-capitalized. Think of the patriotic songs you sing as a citizen of the United States. When you sing "America, the Beautiful" or "My Country, 'Tis of Thee" or "You're a Grand Old Flag," don't you praise your nation as a personified whole, using second-person pronouns to celebrate national values like bravery, liberty, pride, peace, and brotherhood from sea to shining sea? Can you imagine a better way of naming an identity to affiliate with and emulate and, in so doing, create?

The more you humans sing about your favorite political or religious projection and blow up fireworks to celebrate it and have arguments about it on talk radio and cable TV 24/7, the more you wear it on T-shirts and bumper stickers, the more you post about it online and talk about it with your friends, the more you do all these things and more, the more real your political or religious projection becomes in your minds, the more substantial and powerful it becomes, and the more likely your projection will be of ruling the world, or at least your corner of it, at least for a while.

Your worship, your arguments, your attention in a real sense bring your projection to life and make it both real and powerful.

In that way, your personified creations become your own creators, creating the world in which you hope to live.

Don't you see that this is not just a religious phenomenon or a political phenomenon; it's a human phenomenon? What would happen if you accepted this insight rather than fearing it?

Why can't you admit that when you're arguing about your God-concepts, just as when you're arguing about politics, you're really arguing about the way you want to live, the future you desire for yourself and your descendants? Why can't you see that these struggles, whether in religion or in

> I have realized that life begins with birth (naissance), continues with knowledge (connaissance), and ends in gratitude (reconnaissance).
> —Paul Tournier

politics or in philosophy or wherever, are essential to your struggle for survival—essential to your cultural evolution and all that it entails?

And why can't you see that if you give up on this struggle, you are simply giving up on having a say in what future your species will create—for yourselves and for this whole planet that you so thoroughly dominate?

"But wait," I protest. "It sounds like you're suggesting that God is nothing more than a human projection." And then, a strange sense of irony washes over me.

Could this inner guineafowl puffer be the voice of the Holy Spirit within me? "Just a minute. Just a minute!" I respond, afraid that my inner guineafowl puffer will disappear into her cave. "If you are the voice of God speaking within me, I must ask: God, are *you* an atheist?"

The guineafowl pufferfish hovers just outside her cave, her fins fanning gracefully to hold her in place. It becomes clear that she does not plan to answer me, nor does she plan to vanish, and I can almost understand why.

Finally, a thought takes shape, as sleek and slippery as a cutthroat trout. I realize that I can never stop speaking about God, whether or not I use the word, for God is all I ever speak about, all I love, all I seek to save and be saved by.

I look for my invisible suitcase, and for now at least, I cannot find it anywhere. It appears to have gone weightless, floated away, vanished.

HERPETHEOLOGY

Today I've been thinking about something my companions and I experienced at Urbina Bay on Isabela. We experienced it again a few days later on Santa Cruz at the Charles Darwin Research Center and at Rancho Manzanillo, and then again the next day, at the Giant Tortoise Breeding Center near Puerto Villamil.

At each place, we experienced sustained moments of shared, focused attention, so shared and so focused that we forgot ourselves. For significant periods of time, we were drawn out of ourselves into the observation of another, as in another species.

We were thoroughly engrossed by tortoises.

Tortoises standing, walking, mating, eating, sleeping, stretching, yawning, climbing, pooping.

We spoke in hushed tones, overcome by natural reverence.

And I also remember that for a few moments in each place, I detached my attention from observing the tortoises with my companions so that I could observe my companions observing the tortoises. The oddness of it struck me. Tortoises? Really? Tortoises? Gray as a rock and only slightly faster—what could be more boring than this? How can this many people remain this enchanted for this long by tortoises?

And yet, there they were—there *we* were. Intrigued. Drawn in. Enchanted. For minutes, even hours at a time. Whether in the wild or in a breeding center, we surrendered ourselves to them, to their habits, their pace, their well-being, to seeing the world in light of their needs and interests.

We had given our hearts to these unique creatures that are unique features of this unique world.

The great novelist Marilynne Robinson was once asked by an interviewer, "What single thing would make the world in general a better place?"

She replied, "Loving it more."

And then the revelation comes: in loving these unique creatures that are unique features of this unique world, we were making the world better.

I do not doubt this in even one neural synapse of my brain.

I do doubt whether selling another hamburger or computer makes the world better. I do doubt whether erecting another strip mall or website makes the world better. At times, truth be told, I wonder whether giving another lecture or writing another book makes the world better.

But this simple gaze of love from one unique creature to another—I do not doubt the value of this. Dear Charles Darwin himself said that "the most noble attribute of man" is the "love for all living creatures."[23]

It's odd, some will say, to associate tortoises—or any reptiles, really—with love. They exhibit little to no maternal care. The mother tortoise digs a hole, deposits her eggs, buries them, and leaves them. She never checks back on them, and if, by chance, she bumps into one of her progeny 3 or 50 or 150 years later, there's no evidence she would recognize them. (There's one fascinating exception: the

---

23. Charles Darwin, "Comparison of the Mental Powers of Man and the Lower Animals (Continued)" in *The Descent of Man* (New York: D. Appleton, 1875), chap. 4, sec. 126, Wikisource, https://tinyurl.com/yylrfrrr.

Burmese brown mountain tortoise. She builds a mound nest of decaying vegetation, lays her eggs in it, and guards them for some period of time, more like a crocodile than a turtle or tortoise. Of course, eventually they hatch, and from that point they're on their own.)

In my backyard, I keep some red-footed tortoises that have been in my care for nearly thirty years. When they see me, they come running at full speed (*full speed* being a relative term, of course). But I don't think they love me or like me. What they love is food—a watermelon rind or banana peel or mango skin—and they associate me with food. True, a few of them will pause for me to scratch their shell, and even raise and wriggle their butt end a bit to intensify the experience. And if I sit on the grass, a few of them will come, seeking food, and when they see I have none, they will sit down beside me and rest. Perhaps this is, on a reptilian level, an expression of love: accepting me as a benign or even benevolent presence in their world.

The sixteen of us who traveled together on the *Golondrina* were not merely consumers of a particular kind of touristic experience, although we were that. More, we were lovers, "lovers in a dangerous time," as a favorite songwriter (Bruce Cockburn) put it, lovers who because of the danger decided to make the world a better place by slowing down long enough to pay for its improvement—by paying attention, the reverent, even holy attention of love.

I was always amused when overtaking one of these great monsters [a tortoise], as it was quietly pacing along, to see how suddenly, the instant I passed, it would draw in its head and legs, and uttering a deep hiss fall to the ground with a heavy sound, as if struck dead. I frequently got on their backs, and then giving a few raps on the hinder parts of their shells, they would rise up and walk away;—but I found it very difficult to keep my balance.

—Charles Darwin

Our attentive experience of self-forgetfulness and whole-hearted tortoise observation was, in a real way, ecstatic. We were taken out of ourselves in the contemplation of a creature so different from us in many ways, yet like us in others. We had fallen out of our normal concerns and into love, you might say. Or risen into love. Or embarked upon it. Or leapt into it.

Perhaps the old phrase (thanks, Kierkegaard!) "leap of faith," well worn by philosophers and theologians alike, would be better rendered a *leap of love.*

I know that both Jesus and Saint Paul said that our faith would save us. And I get that. But I wonder if it is equally true to say that if we are to be saved, it will not be by faith alone but by love as well. After all, didn't Jesus say that love is the one greatest command, and didn't Paul say that without love, nothing else we have (including faith that moves mountains) amounts to a hill of beans? Maybe love includes as a given the kind of faith that really matters. That would certainly be the case if another voice in the New Testament was correct when he said, without qualification, "God is love, and those who abide in love abide in God, and God abides in them" (1 John 4:16 NRSV).

Could that be why, for about two hundred thousand people each year, it's worth the time and expense to fly to the Galápagos Islands and join one another, and perhaps even join their Creator, in loving these creations, these tortoises, marine iguanas, land iguanas, sea turtles, lava lizards—this bunch of reptiles?

Could this experience of a loving gaze be the holy prize of a holy pilgrimage?[24]

---

24. Richard Rohr speaks repeatedly and reverently of the mutually mirroring gaze he experienced with his beloved black Lab,

Darwin inherited a God-concept that didn't match with the intricacy of plankton, the extinction of species, or the processes of evolution. So did many of us.

If we'd like to bring our God-concepts into better sync with a Creator who makes sense in this particular universe, we'd better face up to this sobering fact: God loves tortoises. And really, God loves reptiles in general. (Not to mention insects, if we judge based on how many species exist: three hundred thousand beetles, seventeen thousand

Venus, in *The Universal Christ* (New York: Convergent, 2019).

butterflies, and five thousand dragonflies, for example, out of over two million insects in total.[25])

Fathom it: For 245 million years, there were zero people around, but lots and lots of reptiles. And because there were no people, there was no religion. No churches. No rituals. No sermons. No holidays. No offerings. No excommunications, fatwas, pedophilia scandals, sleazy televangelists, or holy wars either. (Nor were there religious authors, for that matter.) There were just millions of reptiles, doing their reptilian things, in the presence of whatever truly exists above and beyond and apart from human concepts.

Apparently, God did not say, "Wow. These things are *boring*. What I really need is a prelude. And a narthex. And some juicy excommunications over sexual variation in the human population. And what I wouldn't give for some organ music or a smoking-hot praise band—with literal smoke machines and hellfire preaching! Praise be to me, for my sake let's get these reptiles out of here so we can get some religious primates evolving, fast!"

---

25. I must quickly add that insects are at this moment undergoing a deeply disturbing die-off, with inevitable impacts up and down the food chain. See Jacob Mikanowski, "'A Different Dimension of Loss': Inside the Great Insect Die-Off," *The Guardian*, December 14, 2017, https://tinyurl.com/ya7bbc4g.

No. For 245 million years, and for 99.999 percent of the 66 million years since, God was happy to have a good universe that included neither a single human nor a single religion, but lots and lots *and lots* of reptiles.

Back in the Mesozoic, there were big reptiles like Argentinosaurus, Brachiosaurus, Triceratops, and T. rexes. Plus there were little ones (some with big names) like Chaoyangsaurus, Limusaurus, Mei long, and Micropachycephalosaurus. Apparently, their existence, sans humans, was good and made sense.

Really, it's hard to imagine the age of humans lasting for 245 million years, don't you agree?

For humans to make sense to ourselves, I think we're going to have to rediscover our kinship with the reptiles—and the fish, insects, birds, mammals, and palo santo trees—with which we share the world.

Charles Darwin actually helped us with this. He did so quite elegantly through a diagram, his only diagram in *On the Origin of the Species*. The diagram is properly abstract for a tome of *Origin*'s scholarly importance, with lots of horizontal gridlines and lots of labels like A, B, m^1, k^7, and w^{14}. Fortunately for the nonacademics of the world, the drawing has evolved and is often presented today as a tree of life.

Simple versions of the tree are rooted in the protists, the earliest forms of one-celled life. From there, the trunk divides into the plant branch of the family on one side and the animal branch on the other. (More complex tree diagrams include bacteria, fungi, and many other branches.) The animal side continues branching, until one large section, the vertebrate clan, branches out into fish, amphibians, reptiles, birds, and mammals. There, on one little leafy twig, we humans are perched next to orangutans, chimps, gorillas, and bonobos. Stare at the diagram long enough and you realize two things: first, we're just one tiny twig in a very big tree, and second, Saint Francis was right.

In the late 1850s, Darwin was worried that Alfred Russel Wallace would beat him to publication with a competing theory of evolution, but in a sense, Saint Francis, who died 656 years before Darwin, beat them both. In his beautiful Canticle, he describes how we humans are related to all our kin in the family tree of creation. I've adapted his prayer as a song:

> Be praised, my Lord, through Brother Sun,
> who brings the light of day;
> He's beautiful and radiant, like you!
> Be praised, my Lord, through Sister Moon,
> Through all her sister stars.
> They're luminous and wonderful, like you!
>
> Be praised, my Lord, through Brother Wind
> And Sister Cloud and Storm.

They bring flowers from Mother Earth for you.
Be praised, my Lord, through Brother Bird;
You gave him wings to fly.
He sings with joy and soars up high for you.

Through Sister Water, Lord, be praised;
She's humble, useful, too.
She's precious, clear and pure, O Lord, like you.
Be praised, my Lord, through Brother Fire,
Whose beauty glows at night.
He's cheerful, powerful, and strong, like you.

Be praised through all those who forgive,
The patient, kind, and brave,
Enduring suffering, trial, and pain, like you.
Be praised, my Lord, through Sister Death,
Who will embrace all life,
And carry us up to the arms of you.

I praise and bless you, Lord, and give a grateful
    heart,
To serve and love you, Lord, in humility and joy.[26]

In this grand vision, we aren't ruling from the heights
of a great top-down pyramid or chain of being, generals

---

26. You can listen to and download the song on Bandcamp:
https://tinyurl.com/y59x42ys.

under King God in the divine chain of command. In this grand vision, we aren't given by our rank a carte blanche to dominate, oppress, exploit, and exterminate everything below us. No, we aren't at the top of anything; we're simply at the tip, the tip of one small branch of a very huge, verdant tree, and all created things are our grandparents, cousins, and siblings. We could not exist without them, without plants producing oxygen, without insects spreading pollen, and without other animals turning grass or algae into the protein and fat upon which our species has long depended for sustenance. (I am among those who believe that the human diet of the future should and must be much more plant-dependent, if not exclusively so. But even the strictest vegan will depend on bees and other pollinators, on worms and other aerators, as well as on many other creatures.)

Back in the Galápagos Islands, my companions and I felt this connection as we stared at the tortoises. We were communing with our evolutionary relatives. Instead of butchering them for oil or storing them upside down for a year in the hold of a ship for meat, instead of paving their paradise to put up a parking lot, instead of superheating their climate with gas from our guzzlers, for those few moments, at least, we reverently honored them with our undivided attention and, in so doing, celebrated a long-overdue family reunion.

Now, if I consulted my inner guineafowl puffer, she might say that, all things considered, the addition of humans to the family has been a net loss for the rest of creation, so far at least. I could see her point. We're like the cute baby who is born, grows up too fast, runs away, and breaks bad, only to become a notorious sociopath, stealing from everyone, terrorizing everyone, draining the family's accounts with huge medical and legal bills, all while running the family name into the dirt.

As soon as I admit that, I think of the Noah story in the Bible. Of course, I take the story *literarily* rather than literally, which means I look to it for *meaning*, not facts. And there's an oddly, tragically

> When we try to pick out anything by itself, we find it hitched to everything else in the universe.
>
> —John Muir

meaningful moment in the story when God agrees with my inner guineafowl puffer. God looks around at the world and feels depressed. So much violence. So much oppression. So much harm. Just six chapters into the Bible, and the Creator "saw that the wickedness of humankind was great in the earth, and that every inclination of the thoughts of their hearts was only evil continually. And the Lord was sorry about making humankind on the earth, and it grieved God to God's heart. So the Lord said, 'I will blot out from the earth the human beings I have created . . . for I am sorry that I have made them.'"[27]

In the biblical story (again, not to be taken literally for facts, but literarily for meaning), just ten generations pass (Adam, Seth, Enosh, Kenan, Mahalalel, Jared, Enoch, Methuselah, Lamech, Noah), and humans make a far worse mess of things than all the T. rexes and Utahraptors that ever lived. "Oh, for the days of the reptiles," I can imagine God saying, "when carnivores simply preyed on herbivores without degrading them, enslaving them, torturing them, keeping them in cages and concentration camps, and driving them to extinction. Those were the good old days."

I think back to the tortoises that were rescued from a volcanic eruption on Five Hills at Cerro Azul on Isabela. I remember a large male who was walking around

---

27. Genesis 6:5–7. For reasons that are impossible to justify today, God in the Noah story decides to kill all the innocent with the guilty, including the innocent animals. Like all great literary works, this one has some obvious loose ends. If it's any consolation, God feels sorry again at the end of the story and vows never to do *that* again, creating the rainbow as a reminder, like a proverbial string around the finger.

with a long stalk of grass hanging from his mouth. He didn't have a spouse like mine who could, with the tiniest touch of a finger to her chin, signal that he should wipe his mouth. He looked a little silly, really, but I liked that about him. He didn't care what people thought. He was, after all, not a people. He was a reptile, and his kind have survived a lot longer than us upstart humans.

Dogs, of course, are impressed by us. And cats find us, ahem, occasionally useful. But to reptiles, we're nothing special. And that's why I find it good for my soul to be in their presence. I have to appreciate them for what they are, with no purrs or wagging tails to flatter my ego.

Something I love about where I live in Southwest Florida is that every day, all year long, I'm surrounded by reptiles and their cousins, the amphibians. If I step out my door, I'm greeted by brown anoles and curly-tailed lizards (both nonnative species that are making our native green anoles super rare). If I walk through my yard, chances are I'll see a five-lined skink, black racer snake, or yellow rat snake a few times a month. At night, I'll hear the strange gulping sound of Cuban treefrogs (another nonnative that has replaced our native green and barking treefrogs). A half-dozen native (and threatened) gopher tortoises have dug their burrows in my front yard, invited by my intentional landscaping decision to create suitable habitat with native plants.

And trudging around in my fenced backyard, my own little herd of tortoises thrives: red-footeds and yellow-footeds from South America, Russians from Central Asia, a pair of leopards, and a lone male sulcata from Africa. They wander around munching grass, always alert for a watermelon rind or other vegetative offering I may drop into their world. Every morning and late afternoon, especially after a rain, I'll hear the sound of males mounting females, not the throaty groans of the male Galápagos tortoises, but more the raspy sound of a chain-smoking chicken clucking. If I'm lucky, after supper, as I walk among the mango trees, I may see a female tortoise backed up to a tree trunk, digging a hole with her rear feet, dropping two to eight ping-pong-ball-sized eggs into the nest chamber, then covering them up.

I'll wait until she's finished and then go back with my flashlight to dig up the eggs so they won't become a snack for local raccoons. I'll wash them and put them in an incubator, marking an X with the date and the name of the female on the top. The X will help me not to turn the eggs during their four or five months of gestation, and the name and date will help me keep track of who the mother is and when I should expect the eggs to hatch.

I've witnessed hatchlings emerging from their eggs hundreds and hundreds of times over the years, but still

I'm in awe. The show starts when the egg-bound embryo has grown large and strong enough inside the egg that when she extends her neck, she can cause a crack to appear on the shell, like the mark of a stone on a windshield, but from the inside out. Soon, chips of the hard outer shell flake away, revealing the leathery interior layer. Gradually, the hatchling shifts her body and cracks more and more of the brittle shell, until she eventually cuts through the leathery layer too, using a tiny egg tooth that has formed on her beak for that purpose. A day or two after her initial pip, a little leg or head appears through the leathery layer, and soon the whole top of the shell is broken off, and a little hatchling appears, usually with its yolk attached like a small grape to her plastron. The yolk is gradually absorbed, leaving a temporary mark like a belly button, and the hatchling emerges, blinks, walks around, and looks at me with no affection, no fear, just reptilian detachment.

And I gaze back at the little hatchling.

Because of my evolutionary heritage, I gaze with my uniquely human curiosity, my inheritance from millions of mutations over millions of years. You can call that evolutionary inheritance the image of God if you like. That's how I see it. The ability to see, to notice, to love—surely that is our most God-like quality, or in Darwin's words, "our most noble attribute."

I gaze with human benevolence and with a deeper human awareness, thanks to dear Charles and dear Saint Francis, of our profound, inescapable kinship.

I gaze with love.

And somehow, the world is made a little better.

ORNITHEOLOGY

A sking me whether I love reptiles or birds more is like asking which of my grandchildren I love most. I can't choose.

If my reading list is an indication, though, birds have had the upper hand in recent years. Jennifer Ackerman's *The Genius of Birds* sat on my bedside table for many months, a fascinating read that I didn't want to end. On my flight to the Galápagos, I finished Susan Cerulean's *Tracking Desire: A Journey after Swallow-Tailed Kites*, which is a love story about the impossibly graceful bird species that

If the dynamics of the universe from the beginning shaped the course of the heavens, lighted the sun, and formed the earth, if this same dynamism brought forth the continents and seas and atmosphere, if it awakened life in the primordial cell and then brought into being the unnumbered variety of living beings, and finally brought us into being and guided us safely through the turbulent centuries, there is reason to believe that this same guiding process is precisely what has awakened in us our present understanding of ourselves and our relation to this stupendous process.

—Thomas Berry

has captured her heart, and mine. Right before that, I read Mark I. Wallace's audacious and beautiful *When God Was a Bird: Christianity, Animism, and the Re-Enchantment of the World*. It was a delight of good writing and constructive theology. Before that, I enjoyed Debbie Blue's *Consider the Birds: A Provocative Guide to Birds of the Bible.*

Since returning home, two more bird-oriented books have had my attention. First, I've enjoyed Elizabeth A. Johnson's *Ask the Beasts: Darwin and the God of Love.* She writes:

> One animal more than any other has been used to symbolize the effective presence of the Spirit in the world, namely the Bird. To ancient peoples, these denizens of the skies seemed closer to the heavenly dwelling place of God, and their freedom of riding the wind and coming to rest on earth came to represent the streaming of divine power to land-bound humans. . . . The notion of a warm maternal bird fostering and cherishing the growth of her young, actually engendering them into existence by the loving power of her own body, provides an apt animal metaphor for the creative work of the Spirit of God, Giver of life.[28]

She recounts the image of the dove descending to rest on Jesus in Luke's Gospel (3:22), along with many

---

28. Elizabeth A. Johnson, *Ask the Beasts: Darwin and the God of Love* (London: Bloomsbury, 2014), 139–40.

other appearances of divine-bird imagery in the Hebrew Scriptures:

> Whether hovering like a nesting mother bird over the egg of primordial chaos at the creation (Gen. 1.2); or sheltering those in difficulty under the protective shadow of her wings (Ps. 17.8, 36.7, 57.1, 61.4, 91.4, and Isa. 31.5); or bearing

the enslaved upon her great wings toward freedom (Ex. 19.4; Deut. 32.11–12), the approach of
God's creative and recreative Spirit is evoked with
allusion to this animal and, by association, to the
broad tradition of divine female power.[29]

Several good friends kept telling me that I couldn't
write this book without reading another book about
birds, Jonathan Weiner's *The Beak of the Finch: A Story
of Evolution in Our Time*. Weiner traces the research of
Peter and Rosemary Grant. This husband-wife team has
been studying a small population of Darwin's finches on
Daphne Major in the Galápagos Islands for over forty
years. Daphne Major, despite its name, is a small island
that I did not visit on either of my trips for two reasons:
first, it's notoriously hard to access because it is bordered
by tall cliffs; and second, it's open only to a small group of
scientists, and never to tourists.

Of course, Darwin wasn't anywhere close to realizing
the significance of the local finches during his five-week
visit to the Galápagos Islands in the 1830s. In fact, as we've
already noted, he misidentified the specimens as being
from different families, failing to realize that they were all

---

29. Johnson, *Ask the Beasts*, 139.

related to each other because they were descendants of a common ancestor. His mistake was understandable when you see how different their beaks are.

The warbler finch, for example, has a thin, needle-like beak, which is a perfect tool for snatching insects from foliage. The woodpecker finch's beak is thick and wedge-like, perfectly adapted to extract beetle and termite larvae from beneath the bark of trees. The cactus finch's longer, spike-like beak helps it penetrate cactus flowers and fruits for pollen and seeds, while the three species of ground finches (named for their size—small, medium, and large) have short, thick beaks that equip them for opening the seeds they find scattered among the sand, rocks, and gravel of more arid zones across the islands.[30]

It wasn't until modern DNA analysis that scientists could determine definitively that all thirteen species of Galápagos finches are more closely related to each other than they are to any species on the mainland. That means that one ancestor finch species reached the islands from the mainland in the distant past and evolved over the last few million years into the thirteen species we now see. (Weiner adds that the genetic differences among the thirteen

---

30. For drawings of finch beaks, see Daniel Bernal, *Beak Morphology of Darwin's Finches*, ArtStation, September 2018, https://tinyurl.com/y62dyzzn.

species of finch are about the same as the genetic differences between chimpanzees, orangutans, gorillas, and us.)

The Grants decided to study Daphne Major's population of medium ground finches. The island's small size meant that they could get to know literally every single individual in the population, rising at dawn to stretch mist nets to capture them, then taking measurements—wing length, beak dimensions, weight—and banding them for quick identification. Year by year, their data set grew. During lean years of low rainfall, the population dropped to around three hundred, and during green years of high rainfall, it grew to over a thousand, each identified by the Grants. They could follow one individual, say number 5960, through its whole life, keeping track of which females it mated with, how many offspring it produced, and how many of those offspring survived long enough to reproduce.

For the first four years of their research, there was little change in the birds, but in 1977, an eighteen-month-long drought began. Soon, all the small and medium-sized seeds were gone, leaving only large seeds with thick hulls and spines. Finches with smaller beaks couldn't open those seeds, and many starved. In fact, the population plummeted by over 80 percent during the drought. The Grants would walk among the rocks and collect the dried carcasses, each with a band, each known to the Grants. And that's when their data set suddenly became invaluable: the surviving finches had demonstrably thicker (they used the word *deeper*) beaks. When they measured the beaks of the next generation after the drought, they showed a 4 percent increase in depth—amazing, after just one generation. The numbers demonstrated natural selection.

The Grants continued their research. In 1983, just five years after the drought, an El Niño weather pattern dropped ten times the normal annual rainfall on Daphne Major, and the arid island went from ashy brown to lush green. In particular, some species of fast-growing vines proliferated, vines that produce small seeds. Two years later, another drought struck, and the finches with larger beaks had more trouble picking up the oversupply of small vine seeds, while the finches with the smallest beaks feasted, which enabled them to successfully raise more young, passing on their smaller beak-size to the next generation. The results were again measurable, again demonstrating natural selection.

Jonathan Weiner notes the significance of the word *dynamic* in the title of the Grants' first book, *Evolutionary Dynamics of a Natural Population*:

> "It's important to keep in mind," says Rosemary: "Species don't stand still. You can't 'preserve' a species." Every species is, as the Grants write in

the last words of their book, "constantly changing and capable of further change."[31]

I read those words and think of the photograph I took of a finch on the *Golondrina* in Puerto Ayora harbor, a black blur in between one step and another.

Weiner devotes a rather bracing chapter to what this kind of dynamism means to us as humans. For example, when insects develop resistance to insecticides, or bacteria develop resistance to antibiotics, we can find ourselves facing famines and epidemics that we assumed we were protected from. Meanwhile, if our fishing boats net all the biggest cod, salmon, snapper, or porgy, repeatedly removing them from the gene pool, we can expect the average size of these species to decline along with their numbers. He summarizes: The more pressure we put on a species— whether it's a pest or a food item—the more we push it to evolve. And nowhere is our pressure more widespread and potentially catastrophic than with our raising of the planet's temperature through burning fossil fuels.

Weiner then explores the work of genetic engineers who, very literally, take evolution into human hands.

---

31. Jonathan Weiner, *The Beak of the Finch: A Story of Evolution in Our Time* (New York: Vintage, 2014), Kindle loc 1126 of 1485.

Some of them, Weiner says, call their work "Generation of Diversity," abbreviated as G.O.D. Weiner warns that their work could also be the Generation of Destruction. When our ancestors began burning coal and oil, they had little insight into how those organic compounds came to be in the past. And they had no foresight as to their destructive impact in the future. But now we see, or are beginning to see. Now we understand, or are beginning to understand. Or at least many of us are. Will we rush headlong into similar catastrophes in the decades ahead in regard to genetic engineering, arrogant dunces playing God?

It strikes me: as our brains evolved, we developed the capacity to tell stories, to see events in sequence as related, from simple, linear cause-and-effect relationships to more complex, systemic conditions-and-outcomes relationships. We might say that through this evolutionary adaptation of storytelling, enhanced by cultural evolution, we have developed the ability to see into the past and look into the future.

We have learned to interpret the layers of sediment and the fossils they contain, along with many other scientific data banks that, put together, fill out the story of our past: layers in glacial ice, deposition rings in stalactites and stalagmites, layers in lake-bottom silt, growth rings in trees. And we have learned to predict what, say, raising the carbon content of our atmosphere from 350 parts per million to 450 will mean. In this way, we can now see that evolution doesn't simply happen to us over long periods of time. No, we actively participate in evolution in a thousand ways, when we shoot the largest bucks in the herd or catch the largest cod from the school, when we practice selective breeding or genetic engineering, when we use fossil fuels and heat up our environment—or vote for the fossil fools who deny climate change in spite of all evidence.

We're a lot like the teenage boy who is given his first .22 and runs out to shoot something, anything, just to prove he can do it. In fifteen minutes, he kills a mockingbird, a rabbit,

> The earth beneath my feet is the great womb out of which the life upon which my body depends comes in utter abundance. There is at work in the soil a mystery by which the death of one seed is reborn a thousandfold in newness of life. In the contemplation of the earth, I know that I am surrounded by the love of God.
>
> —Howard Thurman *(adapted)*

and a squirrel, and injures the neighbor's cat. And then he realizes, "Wow. The gun works. I have some power. I can kill stuff. It's easy to do. *I had better be careful.*" His destruction awakens him to his responsibility. Or so we hope.

This brings me back to a morning on Rábida. We had been walking next to the rust-red cliffs on a rust-red beach, and we came upon a dead pelican. Billy gathered us around and said, "The pelican is my favorite bird. I know why it is my favorite. It's because of something that happened to me when I first arrived on the Galápagos Islands from my home in Guayaquil."

He told us how he got his first Galápagos job on a fishing boat. Whenever his fellow fishermen came upon a pelican, they would mercilessly kill it—with an oar, a stick, a rock. Appalled by this cruelty, Billy asked, "Why do you do this to the poor brown pelican?"

The pelican, they explained, eats fish, and it swallows them whole. For that reason, the bird needs very strong digestive juices to reduce fish scales and bone to slurry in its stomach. When it defecates, its waste is so acidic that it burns the paint off of boats. The fishermen hated having to repaint their boats because of corrosive pelican feces, so they decided to kill every pelican they could, for the sake of their paint jobs.

Billy argued with them to stop the cruel practice, but his efforts didn't have much effect until Ecuador imposed stiff fines for harming native wildlife. Although the killing has stopped (or at least slowed), Billy's empathy for the pelicans continues and has evolved into a lifelong love for them.

Darwin himself was shocked by human cruelty to birds when he was on the islands. Because creatures on the Enchanted Isles evolved without fear of humans, it was easy to simply walk up to an animal and kill it. Darwin described watching a boy sit by a well. When finches, mockingbirds, or ground doves came for a drink, the boy simply whacked them with a stick. A warm pile of dead birds soon accumulated at the boy's feet.

I wonder. We humans evolved with—and to a degree, because of—our capacity to kill. To kill food. To kill human rivals and opponents. Even the most dedicated pacifist among us today is the descendant of killers.

And so I wonder if we are capable of evolving beyond our rapacious past. I wonder if we will stop trying to play G.O.D., in the sense of believing that it is our right to take life at our convenience, whether to eat or to protect our paint job or to keep our GDP humming along at a rate that pleases investors.

I think of the dove, that symbol of nonviolence. I think of the story of Jesus at his baptism, as a dove of peace rather than an eagle of empire descended upon him.

And then I think of fishermen clubbing pelicans on Santa Cruz at the very moment Rosemary and Peter

Grant were getting to know the ground finches on Daphne, tenderly extracting one from a mist net, cupping its warm, trembling body in their hands, measuring it, weighing it, banding it, rejoicing when it built a nest and fledged young, noticing and caring when it died during a drought.

I go back and reread Rilke's poem, and I become the falcon, circling the tower of God in ever widening circles. I may not complete this last circle, but I give myself to it.

"The mind is our beak," Weiner wrote, "and the human mind is even more variable than the brain."[32] In other words, our cultural software can evolve even faster than our biological hardware.

If the Galápagos finches survive because of the variability of their beaks, then no doubt what one scientist called our "psychological polymorphism" will play a significant role in our human struggle for survival. As communities of us subject our minds and hearts, our values and vision, our moral imagination and character to intentional cultural evolution, we become new kinds of Christians or Muslims, new kinds of Jews or Buddhists, new kinds of Sikhs or Hindus, new kinds of atheists or humanists

---

32. Weiner, *Beak of the Finch*, Kindle loc 1295 of 1485.

or Canadians or Brits or Nigerians or Cambodians—new kinds of human beings.

Mutants, if you will, who may find a new way of adapting to and occupying our current ecological niche and who may migrate toward a new way of life.

Or not.

ECOTHEOLOGY

I've been back from the Galápagos for over a month now, and I can't stop pondering the persistent, seemingly bottomless sadness of Charles Darwin's later years. His sadness could have been clinical depression, written into his genes. It could have been the secondary consequence of some chronic medical condition, the symptoms of which included severe headaches, nausea, vomiting, and flatulence, which made it highly embarrassing for the proper Victorian gentleman to go out in public.

Love all of God's creation, both the whole of it and every grain of sand. Love every leaf, every ray of God's light. Love animals, love plants, love each thing. If you love each thing, you will perceive the mystery of God in things. Once you have perceived it, you will begin tirelessly to perceive more and more of it every day. And you will come at last to love the whole world with an entire, universal love.

—Fyodor Dostoevsky

His sadness could have been a father's grief after the death of some of his ten children, especially his beloved Annie, who died at the age of ten. It could have been the psychosocial drain of thinking differently from nearly everyone around him, of seeing things that they didn't see—and probably didn't want to see. It could have been the stress of knowing that his writings would earn him hatred and scorn from those who were piously prone to misunderstanding and misjudgment.

It could have been all of the above, and more.

And the "more" could include this: Charles may have foreseen—and feared—where his radical new ideas might lead.

He had reason to fear. During the course of his lifetime, a form of exploitive international capitalism known as imperialism was conquering the world, with European empires struggling like bull elephants to dominate markets, rapaciously extracting global resources and exploiting global labor. The result? War, genocide, slavery, oppression, piracy, and environmental plunder across the colonized world, and especially across what we now call the Global South. The colonization process perfectly epitomized the African proverb "When the elephants fight, it is the grass that suffers the most."

Meanwhile, about twenty miles from Darwin's comfortable manor in Kent, Karl Marx and Friedrich Engels watched from London with moral horror as imperial capitalism concentrated more and more wealth, power, and weapons in the hands of small European superelites. They knew that such a system of gross injustice and growing inequity could not stand. With the proletarian masses struggling for necessities while the elite upper classes hoarded luxuries, the fall of the house of imperial capitalism would be ugly when its time came. In *The Communist Manifesto* (1848), they sought to describe the mechanisms by which the upper classes struggled to maintain their regime of advantage and the exploited masses struggled to topple it.[33]

In a sense, both of the twentieth century's titanic economic ideologies were shaped by two phrases made paramount by Darwin: *the struggle for survival* and *the survival of the fittest*. Capitalism and Marxism disagreed on so much, but they shared these phrases as fundamentals of their creeds.

Obviously, capitalism existed before Darwin, as did experiments in communism (including one in Acts in the New Testament). But after Darwin, both capitalism and communism were reshaped by their use—and abuse—of Darwin's ideas.

At the heart of twentieth-century communism was the sociological struggle for survival of working classes, seeking liberation from the oppression of domineering elites so they could control the means of production and share more fairly in the fruits of their labor. Which population

---

33. Marx and Engels advocated communism as a revolutionary alternative to capitalism. They saw socialism as a reformist compromise between the two. See "Manifesto of the Communist Party," *Marz/Engels Selected Works*, vol. 1 (Moscow: Progress Publishers, 1969), 98–137, on Marxists.org, https://tinyurl.com/opzl2g2.

would outcompete the other, the oppressed proletariat or the oppressive bourgeoisie?[34]

At the heart of industrial-era capitalism was the individual quest for survival, with consumers, workers, and corporations vying with rivals on all sides in a constant struggle of bloody dog-eat-dog competition. Who would be the fittest: McDonald's or Burger King? Ford or Chevrolet? Apple or IBM? You or your neighbor? The American capitalist Andrew Carnegie put it starkly:

> While the law [of competition] may be sometimes hard for the individual, it is best for the race, because it ensures the survival of the fittest in every department. We accept and welcome, therefore, as conditions to which we must accommodate ourselves, great inequality of environment; the concentration of business, industrial and commercial, in the hands of the few; and the law

---

34. Karl Marx said, "Darwin's book is very important and serves me as a basis in natural science for the class struggle in history." And at Marx's graveside, Engels eulogized Marx with a reference to Darwin: "Just as Darwin discovered the law of evolution in organic nature, so Marx discovered the law of evolution in human history." Richard William Nelson, "Darwin on Marx," Darwin Then & Now, April 18, 2010, https://tinyurl.com/y5wujybv.

of competition between these, as being not only beneficial, but essential to the future progress of the race.[35]

Through the Cold War, the two ideologies set themselves up as antagonists in their own struggle for survival, ultimately throwing themselves into an arms race defined by mutually assured destruction, as if to say, "Either one of us survives, or neither of us does!"

In this way, *the struggle for survival* and *the survival of the fittest* framed both capitalism and communism, and defined both the twentieth century and the century that is taking shape in its aftermath: struggle, competition, kill or be killed—that's the way of nature, red in tooth and claw, and there is no alternative.

That phrase, "nature, red in tooth and claw," became an unofficial motto of Darwinian thought, even though it was published nine years before *On the Origin of the Species* and was written not by a scientist but by the poet Alfred, Lord Tennyson. His artful and agonized poem *In Memoriam* seethed with both personal grief and the aggrieved spirit of the times. Tennyson's friend Alfred Henry Hallam had died suddenly in 1833, and Tennyson reflected upon

---

35. Andrew Carnegie, *The Gospel of Wealth, and Other Timely Essays* (New York: Century, 1900), 4.

Hallam's death in the larger context of a world churning with death, exemplified in new geological and archeological discoveries, especially fossils of thousands of species (or types) that had gone extinct. Nature, personified as feminine, simply didn't care:

> "So careful of the type?" but no.
> From scarped cliff and quarried stone
> She cries, "A thousand types are gone:
> I care for nothing, all shall go.
>
> "Thou makest thine appeal to me:
> I bring to life, I bring to death:
> The spirit does but mean the breath:
> I know no more."

How does Tennyson's Christian humanity (rendered masculine in the poem) respond to the heartlessness of nature, especially when Christianity teaches that God the creator is love, light, and life, not carelessness, darkness, and death? In the framing of that question, Tennyson employs the phrase "Nature, red in tooth and claw":

> And he, shall he,
>
> Man, her last work, who seem'd so fair,
> Such splendid purpose in his eyes,
> Who roll'd the psalm to wintry skies,

Who built him fanes[36] of fruitless prayer,

Who trusted God was love indeed
And love Creation's final law—
Tho' Nature, red in tooth and claw
With ravine, shriek'd against his creed—

Who loved, who suffer'd countless ills,
Who battled for the True, the Just,
Be blown about the desert dust,
Or seal'd within the iron hills?

No more?

In this harsh world of violent hunger (the archaic meaning of *ravine*), what's left for idealistic humanity to hope for, to be? What meaning remains when humanity is reduced to the level of dinosaurs (or dragons), struggling in the slime for survival? What hope remains for humans when humans, like dinosaurs, are destined for extinction, their only legacy to be dry dust blowing in the wind or dead fossils buried in hills?

A monster then, a dream,
A discord. Dragons of the prime,
That tare each other in their slime,

---

36. Temples.

Were mellow music match'd with him.

O life as futile, then, as frail!
O for thy voice to soothe and bless!
What hope of answer, or redress?
Behind the veil, behind the veil.[37]

Tennyson, pummeled with existential questions, can only reply with a pious cliché, "behind the veil," implying that in heaven, in the afterlife, it will all make sense, even though right now life seems as futile as it is frail.

That hope, though repeated, rings hollow, like an echo. Tennyson himself said of the poem, "It's too hopeful, this poem—more than I am myself."[38]

I cannot doubt that Darwin, that dutiful, honest, sensitive soul, foresaw how his ideas could be abused by future generations of capitalists and Marxists to justify heartless cruelty. Neither can I doubt that he felt a sucking emptiness lurking in the shadows of his theory, haunting it like a despairing demon. Yes, "there is grandeur in this view of life," but the grandeur flickers like a candle against the

---

37. Alfred, Lord Tennyson, *In Memoriam A.H.H.*, canto 56, The Literature Network, https://tinyurl.com/7llcy5n.

38. From a conversation with James Knowles; see Oliver Tearle, "A Short Analysis of Tennyson's 'Nature Red in Tooth and Claw' Poem," *Interesting Literature* (blog), January 1, 2016, https://tinyurl.com/y6lkymet.

deep dark of terror, the terror that says the logos of the universe is violence, and the telos of violence is death, and the ethos of death is futility, meaninglessness, vanity.

I ponder Tennyson's poem. Then I reread a poem by his contemporary Matthew Arnold, "Dover Beach."[39] And then I reread a poem by their younger American literary counterpart, Stephen Crane, who came of age in a world remade by Darwin:

> A man said to the universe:
> "Sir, I exist!"
> "However," replied the universe,
> "The fact has not created in me
> A sense of obligation."[40]

I ponder what it must have felt like to have the old Christian world fall to pieces, a world as defined and controlled as an aquarium, with God the aquarium keeper, choosing, discarding, arranging, rearranging. In its place, people found themselves in a vast churning sea, full of

---

39. See Matthew Arnold, "Dover Beach," Poetry Foundation, https://tinyurl.com/y8pne328.

40. See Stephen Crane, "A Man Said to the Universe," Poetry Foundation, https://tinyurl.com/y5myp6k2.

frenzied sharks above and haunted by cold, dark, immeasurable depths below.

For a moment, I realize why people hated Darwin so much. He spoke the truth, but the truth was hard, and they preferred their comfortable imaginary aquarium.

I ponder all this, and I remember a contrasting feeling that came over me in my eight days in the Galápagos

> The earth herself, burdened and laid waste, is among the most abandoned and maltreated of our poor; she "groans in travail" (Rom 8:22). We have forgotten that we ourselves are dust of the earth (cf. Gen 2:7); our very bodies are made up of her elements, we breathe her air and we receive life and refreshment from her waters.
>
> —Pope Francis

Islands, not once, but at least a half-dozen times. It was the feeling not of struggle, not of desperation, but of *leisure*.

I felt it when I watched, on island after island, hundreds of marine iguanas lying on the rocks, occasionally sneezing out some salt, occasionally repositioning their bodies to catch more sunlight or arrange more shade. Even when I had that joyful afternoon on Fernandina snorkeling with them as they fed on algae underwater, they reminded me of cows grazing in a field, placid, at ease, at peace. The supply of food was endless, carpeting every rock. They had no hurry, no worry, no stress. If Jesus had walked the Galápagos, I can imagine him saying, "Consider the marine iguanas on the shore. They do not toil, nor do they spin."

I felt the same sense of leisure when I watched sea lions playing, sleeping, nursing, playing, sleeping, nursing, and occasionally catching fish at sea. There was no shortage of fish. There was no shortage of safe places to snooze and snore. For them, life was not a bitch but a beach.

I felt it with the tortoises of Urbina Bay and Rancho Manzanillo. They could go a year without food, we were told, but here they were, living in a salad bar, literally surrounded with bounty. They could afford to move slowly, munch slowly, live at a tortoise's pace, because life required so little struggle for them.

I also felt it in the ghost forests of palo santo trees. They were suited to their environment, wet or dry. They were not struggling for survival, even in that seasonally arid place.

Now look, I know this isn't the whole story. I know that when an El Niño weather system hit the islands in 1982–83, between 55 and 70 percent of the iguanas on some of the islands died, and in another El Niño in 1997–98, mortality reached 90 percent. The year after an El Niño, there is almost no reproduction because the survivors are too emaciated to produce eggs. Sea lions are similarly affected; in some El Niño years, virtually no babies are born, and of those that are born, virtually none survive, and many adults die too.

But I also know that within a few years, these devastated populations rebound, and in normal years, they live not in constant struggle but in constant bounty. Their lives are not, most of the time, characterized by struggle, but rather by leisure, abundance, and—can I say it?—*joy*! I saw it on the Galápagos Islands, and I see it now that I'm back home.

Of course there is death. Death is part of life for all creatures, including us. And of course there is struggle, and of course there are times of intense, *agonized* struggle. But we live in a world bathed in sunlight, awash in energy, a world brimming with vitality, a world full of opportunity and bounty. There is more than enough, right here, right now. We would see it more clearly and we would enjoy it more dearly if we weren't being driven by an anxious and suicidal narrative that tells us to make war, not love; to make a hasty profit, not durable peace; to compete, not collaborate; to seek winning, not well-being; to seek self-interest, not the common good.

I can't help but wonder: Could our economic systems—whether leaning toward Marx and Engels on the left or Smith and Keynes on the right—have programmed us to reduce Darwin's rich theory to slogans like *the struggle for survival*, *the survival of the fittest*, and *nature, red in tooth and claw* for their own benefit? Could it be that these systems need us to frame life in those desperate terms of perpetual scarcity, so that we will produce, produce, produce? Isn't that what all contemporary economic systems need us to do most—like anxious drones, to produce, consume, produce, consume, until we exhaust ourselves and die?

Against this backdrop of anxiety and pressure, the biblical call to Sabbath feels truly revolutionary. *Labor* doesn't have the last word: *leisure* does.

The truth is, Darwin's key phrase was neither *the struggle for survival* nor *the survival of the fittest*. Darwin's interest was descent, or transmutation, or evolution *by natural selection*.

Natural selection was Darwin's big idea.

That key phrase only changed when Darwin's younger counterpart, Alfred Russel Wallace, wrote to Darwin and said he felt it overly personified nature, as if nature were actively choosing or selecting winners and losers. Wallace recommended an alternative phrase used by Herbert Spencer in his writings on economics, *survival of the fittest*, and Darwin, ever humble and open to new data, agreed that it was a better term and began using it (eventually adding it as the subtitle to *On the Origin of the Species*.)

Unfortunately, if *natural selection* was open to misunderstanding, so was *survival of the fittest*, but in a more dangerous way. Darwin and Wallace thought of *fitness* like a puzzle piece: something is fit when it fits in with the local environment. The fittest are those who fit into their local environment most harmoniously, naturally, and fully. The subtitle could have been *Survival of the Most Harmonious*.

But in the hands of both capitalists and Marxists, *fit* came to be understood as athletic, strong, fast, tough, aggressive, powerful, dominating. So the toughest CEO survives. The most ruthless corporation survives. The most vicious and competitive politician wins the election and rules the nation. The most aggressive movement, army, party, ideology, or dictator kills off its competition and survives. A contemporary global strongman perfectly articulated this view in a recent tweet:

> The weak crumble, are slaughtered and are erased from history while the strong, for good or for ill, survive. The strong are respected, and alliances are made with the strong, and in the end peace is made with the strong.[41]

But again, we must realize this obsession with superior strength wasn't what Charles (or Alfred) meant by *survival of the fittest*. Not even close. Just as capitalistic interpreters read the Bible through capitalistic lenses, so do they read Darwin. They see what they want to see. They see the only thing their economics and politics allow them to see: a carte blanche for greed, rapaciousness, unbridled self-interest, and unrestrained competition and pursuit of power.

Medieval Christianity certainly had totalitarian tendencies, but nothing like the totalitarianism of modern capitalism and communism.

---

41. The Office of the Prime Minister of Israel (@IsraeiliPM), Twitter post, August 29, 2018, 10:05 a.m., https://tinyurl.com/y5zlrd67.

It's true, inter- and intra-species competition does play a role in natural selection. But ruthless kill-or-be-killed competition is neither the only nor the most important component of the process. Instead of *survival of the most ruthless*, we would be truer to Darwin, Wallace, and the biological revolution they unleashed to say *survival of the best adapted*. The individuals and species that are best adapted to their environment, the individuals and species that can live most harmoniously in their environment— they are the ones that live long enough to reproduce, thus ensuring the survival of their kind.

In addition to **survival of the best adapted**, there are, as I've come to understand the theory, at least five other core elements of natural selection as presented by Darwin and reinforced by over a century of additional research.

Survival of the most adaptable. What happens when a species is well adapted to one environment but that environment changes? When asteroids hit, when sea levels rise and fall, when ocean currents and climate patterns change, when continental plates shift, collide, and separate, when species migrate to a new niche, the individuals and species that are most adaptable are the ones that survive. In other words, in times of change, adaptability, the ability to make new adjustments, becomes more important than past adaptations. Even in stable times, adaptable species don't simply have to compete with other species in their

> We have a new perception of Earth as a vast community of which we are members. As members, we are responsible for assuring that all other members and factors—from the energy balance of soil and air through microorganisms and up to the races and to each individual person—may live on it in harmony and peace.
>
> —Leonardo Boff

native niche to survive; they can enter and adapt to new niches where they will face little or no competition, which explains why life expands to inhabit nearly every niche across the globe.

Survival of the most attractive. Darwin saw the powerful role attraction played in reproduction, both in plants and in animals. In plants, the brightest flowers attract the most pollinators and the sweetest fruits attract the most animals to eat and distribute their seeds. In animals, the most attractive males attract females (or vice versa). Sexual selection helps produce much of the natural world's beauty, from the peacock's multicolor tail to the caribou's impressive antlers to the mockingbird's garrulous song.

Survival of the most diverse. Darwin saw that a population's ability to develop, sustain, and harness the power of difference proved to be one of the most significant survival strategies of all. He explored this dimension of natural selection at a challenging time in his family's life.

In 1856, Emma gave birth to her tenth and last child, Charles Waring, who was developmentally disabled. Were he born today, he would probably have been diagnosed with Down syndrome. He died of scarlet fever at only eighteen months old, and the baby's death left another great wound in his father's already-wounded heart.

Perhaps coincidentally or perhaps not, in 1857, the year after Charles Waring's birth, Darwin became interested in worker bees. Worker bees are sterile, and often make up 98 percent of the individuals in a hive. Why would such huge numbers of sterile individuals be of value, if the only goal of the survival game was reproduction? Wouldn't their sterility be evolutionarily disqualifying? Wouldn't sterile individuals be a drag on the well-being of the whole? Of course not, Charles realized. Evolution isn't simply about individuals; it's about the groups, families, hives, populations, and communities upon which individuals depend. Those sterile worker bees contribute something more important than reproduction to the hive. Their sterility is an expression of diversity, and diversity makes possible a division of labor, and that division of labor makes possible greater adaptability and expanded possibilities for the survival of the community. Intra-species diversity naturally leads us to two additional dimensions of natural selection.

Survival of the best organized. Darwin realized that many species such as bees, ants, and humans deployed their diversity through complex social structures. This complexity allowed them to be more highly adaptable, greatly enhancing their survival.

Survival of the most cooperative. Darwin and later evolutionary biologists have been amazed to discover how different species have co-adapted over time, developing

> We must consciously evolve; we must orient our being toward new life and growth because the unity that we really are, the deep connective tissue of oneness, will not let us rest with separateness. Too much is at stake now to hide behind our secure walls.
>
> —Ilia Delio *(adapted)*

symbiotic relationships that mutually enhance their survival: cows and the bacteria that help them digest grasses; trees and the fungi that connect and nourish their root systems; plants and pollinators; sea anemones and clownfish; even the Mola mola and the cleaner wrasses that eat their parasites. This mutualism is the very opposite of competition, and ecologists are beginning to see the far-ranging dimensions of mutualism in whole ecosystems.

Evolutionary theory now has a bridge to ecological theory, and ecological theory brings us full circle to realize (finally) that human economies are activities that take

place in an environment. Any organism that does not fit harmoniously in its environment will end up as a fossil, as dust blowing across a desert—including the people who submit their brains and chain their lives to inflexible ideologies like contemporary communism and capitalism.

Both systems, after all, arose in the industrial era, an era that produced short-term wealth measured only in money, first by plundering the long-term and multifaceted wealth of the earth, and second by exploiting the labor of vulnerable people. Even though the two systems differed in their plans for distributing that wealth, they shared more assumptions than they realized, assumptions that may not be adaptable to the postindustrial, ecological civilization that we humans must create if we are to survive. To fashion that civilization, we must pay increasing attention to long-term environmental health measured in well-being, not just short-term wealth measured in money, and we must learn to cooperate with our fellow humans, our fellow species, and the physical systems of the earth itself for the common good. We can call this new cooperative economy anything we want to: ecological capitalism, reformed capitalism, organic capitalism, organic Marxism.[42] Whatever we call it, if we don't

---

42. See Philip Clayton and Justin Heinzekehr, *Organic Marxism: An Alternative to Capitalism and Ecological Catastrophe*

develop an economy and a civilization that fit our environment, we simply won't survive.

Perhaps I'm stretching things, but I have to allow Jesus to get a word in edgewise here. I can't help but hear him say of the dominant and anxious economic empires of our day:

> Therefore I tell you, do not worry about your life, what you will eat or what you will drink, or about your body, what you will wear, or about the GDP, whether it is heading up or down. Is not life more than food, and the body more than clothing, and well-being more than the value of your stock portfolios? Look at the marine iguanas on the black volcanic rocks; they neither sow nor reap nor gather into barns, and yet the Creator, working through the harmonious and bountiful ecosystem of creation, feeds them. Are you not of more value than they? And can any of you by worrying add a single hour to your span of life? And why do you worry about clothing?

(Claremont, CA: Process Century, 2014). We need scores of daring economists to defect from current economic orthodoxies and engage in a similar re-visioning of capitalism, before it's too late.

Consider the guineafowl pufferfish of the reef, how she thrives; she neither invests in growth funds nor runs her economy on fossil fuels, yet I tell you, even the sexiest movie star, the wealthiest athlete, and the most powerful politician, in all their self-congratulatory glory, aren't as beautiful as she. Look, if God makes beautiful the fish on the reef, which are alive today and may die in the next El Niño event, will God not much more take care of you—you micro-faiths? So listen: stop worrying, saying, "What will we eat?" or "What will we drink?" or "What is the GDP forecast?" For the economic exploiters and environmental plunderers strive for all these things. But the Creator, through the amazing evolutionary processes that surround you, gave you life and knows what you need.

You need a higher, deeper, and wiser ambition than the competitive drive trumpeted by this suicidal economy. Seek first and foremost to fit harmoniously within the just and bountiful ecosystem of God, and everything you need will be given to you as well.

Really. I mean it. Don't let anxiety drive you into a life of ruthless competition in the tooth-and-claw struggle for survival of the most aggressive. That game is over. Learn to live in the real world, the world of marine iguanas, Galápagos finches, and guineafowl pufferfish. That's the way to live, today and always.

AFTERWORD:
PLAY

I tally the weeks since returning from my Galápagos journey. My adventure has not yet ended. I am still propelled, beckoned, moved, shaken, inspired by what I experienced.

Six weeks after returning, I spoke at a retreat in one of my favorite places, Ring Lake Ranch, near Dubois, Wyoming. Rather than finches and boobies or tortoises and iguanas, I enjoyed the company of cutthroat trout and horses, green-tailed towhees and pine siskins, western bluebirds and Clark's nutcrackers. Just as the geotheology of volcanism and ocean currents fascinated me in the Galápagos Islands, in Wyoming I was intrigued by glaciation, uplift, and erosion. I recalled the crude graffiti of Tagus Cove as I pondered, in profound contrast, the mysterious

petroglyphs inscribed at Ring Lake over a thousand years ago by the Mountain Shoshone.

One afternoon, after a splendid morning of fly-fishing, I was sitting in a rocking chair on the porch of Cabin 8A, watching the late afternoon sun roll glittering diamonds across a blue glacial lake in a hot, dry, late-summer breeze. I felt myself fall into that magical quiet that amplifies soft sounds. Across the lake, an occasional car was barely audible, not the engine, but the sound of its tires on a dusty gravel road, coming, coming, going, gone. A magpie squawked from a distant tree, a chipmunk squeaked from a nearby boulder, three western bluebirds quarreled briefly in midair in front of me, a rufous hummingbird buzzed by from left to right, and then, off to my right, I could hear the faint liquid whisper of stream water tumbling over stones a quarter mile away.

As I rocked slowly in that chair in the pleasant Wyoming sun, I recalled that old suitcase of religious anxiety that used to be such a familiar companion and now seemed distant, like the fading memory of an old, failed relationship. I recalled the wisdom of my inner guineafowl puffer and those two words that accompanied me to the Galápagos Islands: *survival* and *graduation*. I picked up my Galápagos journal and a pen and wrote, tenderly and with surprise:

> I have survived my exodus from conservative, nostalgic, fear-ridden religion. I have graduated into the next grade, with its new courses, assignments, and learning objectives.

Here's more from my musings that afternoon:

> Exodus . . . I am simply in a different place now. It's hard to believe that I used to fear the power

and threats of the gatekeepers of conservative religion, that I used to feel a heavy obligation to defend its supremacy, that I used to find its arguments convincing . . . or intimidating . . . or even interesting. The leash has been cut; the collar is off. I might as well remember making bricks in Egypt. My migration has been long, often agonizing, sometimes intense and other times tedious, but that passage is over, and I feel free. I have come to the other side of the river, the other side of the desert. I am in a different place now. Yes, a promised land of sorts, a land flowing with clear water and the scent of sagebrush. Problems here? Yes, of course. But new ones. For me, better ones.

Graduation . . . I have studied hard, failed and passed many tests, enjoyed my classmates and teachers (usually), and learned all I could from my heritage, although I will always remain open to learning more. I evolved, am evolving, and I am no longer of the species I once was. Of course I'm not finished. To be alive, to be human is to be a blur, between one step and the next. Faith? It's still here, deep within me, as open hands reaching forward. Love for Jesus? Deeper than ever, less pressured, more free. Belief in good news of great joy for all people? Stronger now, surer now, though

> Keep close to Nature's heart and break clear away, once in a while, and climb a mountain or spend a week in the woods. Wash your spirit clean.
>
> —John Muir *(adapted)*

understood differently. I don't care what you call me. A liberal heretic or apostate? If it makes you feel better, label away. A Christian? That's fine, but only if you see solid evidence in my life. A human being? Even better.

It's odd. I always thought that one was a human first, and then added Christian identity on top of it. Now the order flips, and I see the purpose of Christian faith, and other faiths as well, as helping people to become more fully human, fully alive, fully members of the planetary neighborhood we share with all other creatures, all our relations.

Whatever God is, whatever the Spirit is, whatever light and life and logic were radiant in the life of Jesus, that is what I see and love in this beautiful world . . . in those Pacific waves in the Galápagos Islands crashing on black volcanic rocks, in marine iguanas, serene as they graze on algae in cold seawater and then bask in warm sunlight, snorting salt . . . in playful sea lions cavorting with strange masked snorkelers . . . in the snorkelers themselves, so eager to see and savor and connect, laughing aloud through their snorkels. And it is what I feel here in this Wyoming sunlight warming this skin right now.

The physical adventures of this summer, I realize, have given shape to the spiritual journey of my life.

If that isn't the definition of a pilgrimage, what is?

The other day, I came across a quote from Saint Augustine, a theological giant in the Christian tradition about whom I have strongly mixed feelings. I'm sure I had read this passage before, but this time it grabbed me and wouldn't let me go:

Late have I loved you, O Beauty ever ancient, ever new, late have I loved you! You were within me, but I was outside, and it was there that I searched for you. In my unloveliness I plunged into the lovely things which you created. You were with me, but I was not with you. Created things kept me from you; yet if they had not been in you, they would not have been at all. You called, you

shouted, and you broke through my deafness. You flashed, you shone, and you dispelled my blindness. You breathed your fragrance on me; I drew in breath and now I pant for you. I have tasted you, now I hunger and thirst for more. You touched me, and I burned for your peace.[43]

---

43. From one of Richard Rohr's daily meditations, which cites the source as *Confessions*, 10.27, taken from the Office of Readings on St. Augustine's feast day (August 28), https://tinyurl.com/yxf8cl54 and https://tinyurl.com/y4wp4ru7.

"You were within me," he says, "but I was outside." Odd language for those of us who were raised to think that God was absent from within until we had "accepted" God into our hearts. Augustine the outsider listens to the loveliness of the outside world and discovers God calling and shouting through the songs of birds and the crashing of the surf. He looks around the outside world and sees God flashing in the silver scales of a fish, shining in a crescent moon, radiant in the ambers, golds, and greens of a summer meadow. He takes a deep breath, and there God is again, in the sharp scent of pine needles in humid air, the citrus tang of an orange grove, the sweet, subtle aroma of soil in rain. And when he sips red wine, breaks open a warm loaf, and bites into a crisp apple, there God is again, and he becomes hungry and thirsty for more. If hearing, sight, smell, and taste weren't enough, even in the touch of a lover, he feels God arousing him and igniting his passion.

So the outside world beckons the seeker to find God within, and simultaneously to see God as the larger reality in which both outside and inside are held and loved. And what name can he give to that larger embracing reality? "O Beauty," he says, "ever ancient, ever new." I recall another passage from the *Confessions* (10.6) in which the word *beauty* plays a similarly pivotal role. Augustine speaks of observing the earth, the sea, the animals, the winds, the sun and moon, the stars. His attention, he says, implied a restless question, and "their answer was their beauty."

With Augustine's confession in mind, I close my eyes and return in my memory to the beauty of the Galápagos Islands. That sea-lion pup at Rábida comes shooting in front of me, right to left, left to right, fast like a bullet, more graceful than any gymnast. He circles around behind me, shoots away in front of me, and then, impossibly arching

Humans are forgetting that the universe and the Earth are not the result of their creativity or their will. They were not present at the birth of the universe, nor did they set the arrow of time, nor did they invent the primordial energies that continue to stir in the vast evolutionary process and are acting in human nature itself as part of the universal nature. Humans are the last to arrive at the enormous creation party.

—Leonardo Boff *(adapted)*

his back and thrusting with his flippers, he zips back toward me, as if yanked by a huge elastic band. At the last instant he stops, and his face is in my mask, his big, wet, brown eyes meeting mine through the glass. I can count his whiskers.

His eyes have the same look as all the dogs I've ever loved, eyes that plead, "Come on, human! Let's play! Let's play!"

What a miracle play is. It's surely one of life's most underrated phenomena. It's certainly not only a human behavior. If we took time to notice, we'd see that at least some birds play, and so do so many of our fellow mammals.

I've come to see religion as, among other things, all-ages play. We dress up. We play roles. We read our parts. We pretend. At its best, there is an intense recovery of childhood in it, as Jesus said. In acknowledging the playfulness of religion, I'm not trivializing it, because play is serious business.

I was watching my youngest granddaughter the other day, just two years old. She took a picture book and sat in the middle of a rug. She dutifully pointed her finger at words that she cannot read and started talking, weaving improvised phrase to phrase. A year ago, she was making sounds, nonsense sounds, speaking in infant tongues, playing at speech. Ten years from now, she'll sit in the driver's seat of a car, holding the wheel, touching her feet to the pedals, playing at driving. In each of these cases, playful pretending is the warm-up for the real thing.

But here's what I see as I watch my grandchildren: It's not just warm-up for the real thing. It's part of the real thing itself. When the otter slides down a river bank, then climbs again only to slide again, that's not preparing for being an otter; that's utter otter-ness. When a dolphin surfs in a boat wake, when a dog brings his ball and dares me to take it away, when a child sends little chips of wood down a stream, they aren't simply preparing for something else in life: they are living.

Vacations, holidays, trips, adventures—we too often put them in the same frivolous class as play. We contrast them with the serious business of work. We account for them as an expense, maybe even a frivolous luxury, in contrast to the serious necessity of earning money, making investments, or making a living. We justify them because they refresh us so we can get back to work. Indoctrinated by the slave-driving propaganda of our consumptive, competitive economies, we feel guilty for taking a few days off to spend some of that money we've earned in the interests of making a meaningful and joyful life.

I imagine a face-palming, eye-rolling Pharaoh yelling at Moses: "What? Your God wants your people to take a day off? Several days off? To do nothing productive?

To take a little trip into the country? Just to ponder or celebrate the mystery and meaning of life? Look, I don't know about your God, but I am a serious man. I have serious pyramids to build and serious wars to win and serious larders to fill, and you want to go away on a little holiday?

> Soil, water, mountains: everything is, as it were, a caress of God.
>
> —Pope Francis

You've got to be kidding me. Grow up, man. This is the real world! I'll teach you to appreciate just how lucky you are to have a steady job in my glorious enterprise: from now on, you'll have to make bricks without straw!"

You may work for a pharaoh, or within a pharaonic economic system. You may be pressed by duties: needy kids, elderly parents, your own illnesses and struggles. Getting away to remote islands may indeed be a luxury you cannot afford right now, or maybe ever.

But look at what you've just done. You've just withdrawn from the rat race to read this book. You didn't get paid to read it. Nobody told you that you had to read it. You just did it—for fun. For joy. For play. To ponder and celebrate the meaning of life. To refresh and renew yourself. You just indulged in an inner vacation or holiday of sorts, taken through your imagination. You've embarked on a journey, taken yourself on an adventure, word by word, page by page. You've given me the honor of being your companion, but you made this choice and you took this literary voyage on your own.

In so doing, you defied those who measure life by financial profit alone. You defected from all narratives or conceptual models that reduce life to mechanics or economics, that elevate money-making work as profitable and render life-giving play trivial.

Perhaps someday you will make that flight to Baltra and begin your own Galápagos adventure.

But really, the destination is far less important than the loving attention, the mindful openness, and the playful pace you bring with you next time you walk out your own front door right where you live.

Right now, you live in a remarkable place, a place with a remarkable story. Outside your window, just down the street, just outside of town, amazing creatures wait to astound you right now. Believe me, the local song sparrow, mockingbird, American robin, and house wren that you've been hurrying past your whole life have songs that will make your heart sing, if you pause to really listen. Believe me, honeybees and lightning bugs and spring

peepers and common newts live not far from you, and they will amaze you, really amaze you, if you take time to notice. And believe me, the place where you live is as full of stories as any tourist destination. It just takes a bit of curiosity to learn what those stories may be.

Right now, all around you, historic dramas continue to unfold, with plunderers plundering, resisters resisting, and saviors saving the ecosystem around you. That ecosystem was once as pristine as the Galápagos Islands before humans arrived. With less than twenty minutes of internet work, you could find out what species of animals or plants are going extinct in your neighborhood right now. You could learn which local streams and forests that took uncountable thousands of years to develop are in danger of being bulldozed in an afternoon by so-called developers. You could join or help form your local version of the Charles Darwin Research Center, and you could become one of the heroes who steps in to help save what is threatened right now with extinction, right where you are.

And at the very least, you could appreciate what remains. You could make this wounded world better by loving what's left.

Tonight, if you look up, you'll see the moon, maybe Venus, maybe Orion, reminding you that you're riding the wave that began with the big bang 13.7 billion years ago. If you make it your habit to slow down for just a half a minute between your front door and your car or between your office and the subway, so you look up and take a few deep breaths and see with those amazing eyes that you have, who knows what wisdom might dawn upon you during that intentional mini-vacation of twenty-seven seconds?

You are in the midst of an amazing saga of evolution.

You are part of the unfolding, the awakening, the infinite adventure.

Beauty abounds, answering your questions.

Your journey has begun, and you have embarked.

You have eyes to see and a part to play.

APPENDIX:
USING THIS BOOK IN A STUDY GROUP, CLASS, OR RETREAT

If you enjoyed this book, you may want to invite a group of friends to read it and discuss it together. You might share a drink or a meal as you talk.

You can read a chapter or two per week and meet for conversation, or you can read the entire book and then meet to discuss it as a whole. When you gather, you can use these questions to get the conversation going.

1. What sentence or paragraph most struck you? (Read the sentence or paragraph to the group.) Why is it significant to you?
2. What experiences or memories from your life came to mind as you were reading?

3. Did your reading make you feel grateful for anything? What other strong emotions surfaced as you read?

4. Did your reading make you eager to do something, try something, learn more about something, or protect something?

5. What do you care about more as a result of reading this book (or chapter) and being part of this group?

Because this book is about an adventure in the outdoors, a great way to conclude your gatherings would be to plan an outdoor adventure of your own. Consider going camping, kayaking, canoeing, or hiking together. Consider hiring a fishing guide, naturalist, or birding expert to take you on an expedition, or look up a local hiking group or branch of the Audubon Society. Visit a park or museum or nature center. If you've never taken a mindful walk, try this: Walk together in your neighborhood for ten minutes without speaking. Just notice what surrounds you. Then, take ten minutes to share what you noticed and thought about, walking in groups of two or three. You can repeat the process as many times as you want.